D1110046

THE MUTINY AT BRANDY STATION
THE LAST BATTLE OF THE HOOKER BRIGADE
A Controversial Army Reorganization,
Courts Martial, and the
Bloody Days That Followed

To Doug Cope –
hope you enjoy the
Boston connection
Fred Arner

Frederick B. Arner

Bates and Blood Press
Kensington, Maryland

Published by

Bates and Blood Press
10310 Greenfield Street
Kensington, MD 20895

Copyright © 1993 Frederick B. Arner
All rights reserved

Text quoted from *The Wilderness Campaign* by Edward Steere (The Stackpole Company, Harrisburg, Pa.: 1960) is reproduced with the permission of Stackpole Books. *The Civil War Letters of General Robert McAllister,* edited by James I. Robertson, (Rutgers, The State University: copyright © 1965) is reproduced with permission from Rutgers University. Other books quoted with permission include *Fallen Leaves: The Civil War Letters of Major Henry Livermore Abbott* (Kent University Press: 1991); *If It Takes All Summer* by William D. Matter (University of North Carolina Press, Chapel Hill, NC: 1988); *The Civil War, A Narrative, Vol. 3, Red River to Appomattox* by Shelby Foote (Random House, New York: 1974); and *Touched with Fire—Civil War Letters and Diary* [of Oliver Wendell Holmes], edited by Mark DeWolfe Howe (Harvard University Press: 1947).

Maps by Charthouse
Canaan, New Hampshire

Printed in the United States of America

Library of Congress Card Catalog Number: 93-73405

ISBN: 0-9638523-4-5

Table of Contents

Dedicated to the memory of

Colonel William Blaisdell
Captain Henry N. Blake
Private Samuel L. Blood
11th Massachusetts Volunteer Infantry

Foreword

The trapped Spartans never questioned it, even as they savagely fought to their destruction at Thermopylae. And neither did the legions of Rome, nor Hannibal's infantry, nor the Mongols of Genghis Khan. As armies have marched across the pages of history, the battalions of the rank and file have never doubted and and rarely challenged the ancient military premise that their first soldierly function is to follow orders without question. Commanders lead, soldiers obey—whether they like it or not. But sometimes generals can go too far.

During the winter of 1863-1864, the soldiers of the Army of the Potomac rested quietly in their sprawling winter cantonment radiating outward and centered around the little Culpeper County, Virginia, hamlet of Brandy Station, a way-station situated hard by the strategic Orange and Alexandria Railroad. Just north of the little village, on a distinct knoll alongside Fleetwood Hill, the commander of this battered army, Maj. Gen. George Meade, mulled over the condition of things. Meade believed, considering the enormous casualties his forces had suffered during the grueling summer of 1863, that a sweeping reorganization of the army was desirable. In March 1864, Gen. Meade therefor ordered the Army of the Potomac to be reduced from five separate corps and the troops consolidated into three remaining corps, abolishing the I and III Corps in the process. In wholesale fashion, divisions, brigades and regiments were ensconced under new commands and unfamiliar commanders. Many units were eliminated. George Meade had not counted upon the swift and angry reaction to his decree. The bulk of the army was instantly outraged, and rumblings of discord rolled and boiled like so much hot coffee by the campfires scattered about the frozen Virginia countryside.

One period historian characterized a soldier's identity with his unit as "a sacred thing." The writer of this foreword agrees with that observation as he can yet today recall—painfully—the dreadful moment in a rice paddy south of Da Nang when a shot-up Marine rifle company was gathered together by its dejected commander in a pelting rain and disbanded, we survivors conveyed like mere chattel to other regiments. Did our Viet Nam leaders even care that "Delta Company" ceased to exist and we who had endured were now without homes and friends in a strange, hostile land? Did George Meade realize the human and emotional impact of his perfunctory edict? The hero of Fred Arner's book, Capt. Henry N. Blake, reported the reorganization of the northern army "resembled the breaking-up of a family"—and so it was.

After entering the third year of battle, the Army of the Potomac was not comprised of men who had vainly offered combat. These foot soldiers in blue, albeit badly led at times, nevertheless had courageously given their hearts and their bodies to the knife—these men did not have qualms about dying for their country—indeed, they had done so in droves. But during periods of military disappointment and tragic loss, the one thing these men could always count upon as refuge was their unit, i.e., their company, regiment, brigade, division and corps. That identity now disappeared for many affected troops, and their resulting fury knew no bounds. Some chose to protest to the army's leadership, knowing they would encounter heavy odds. The challenge was not refused.

Fred Arner's outstanding research provides understanding to a mostly over-looked but crucial dynamic within the much-troubled Army of the Potomac—that of the loss to many of their all-important unit identity just prior to the crucial Overland campaign. Mr. Arner surfaces a long-forgotten but significantly relevant court martial that dramatically illustrates the depth of feeling and tumult within the army over this signal and transcendental event. Through a painstaking, detective-like investigation, Mr. Arner tracks the drafting by III Corps officers of resolutions objecting to the reorganization, while introducing us to the players of this fascinating judicial episode at Brandy Station, defendants and judges alike. And in also giving a public airing to the insightful and delightfully caustic comments of one of the Civil War's most able scribes, trial defendant Captain Henry N. Blake, 11th Massachusetts Volunteers, Mr. Arner performs a valuable historical service. Captain Blake quite obviously was nobody's patsy, and refreshingly said and wrote just what he meant, no matter the ruffled feathers of some "damn rascal."

In providing a poignant perspective to the outcome of the court martial, the author follows several court martial participants into the faded gloom of the Wilderness, where many inevitably perished, including Brig. Gen. Alexander Hays and a divinely gifted young officer who would have been a star in any army, Major Henry Abbott, 20th Massachusetts Volunteers. We also learn of the brief career of an ordinary and very typical soldier, Private Samuel L. Blood, an infantryman who would have been lost to the archives of history had not his descendant, the author, rescued him from obscurity and compelled us all to be aware and appreciative of Private Blood's uncomplaining sacrifice to his country.

At Brandy Station harsh justice was meted out to those who dared question that a soldier's duty is but to obey. The military rule of law prevailed, as since ancient times, and the men of a grumbling army took their places in new and unaccustomed ranks. But even today historians debate whether the excessively large corps conceived by the reorganization served Meade and Ulysses Grant well in the campaign to follow. Certainly these large bodies of men proved difficult to maneuver in the thickets of central Virginia in the months to follow. Strategic considerations aside, the demoralized soldiers who crossed the Rapidan with alien units into the Wilderness on May 4, 1864, sadly recognized that they left more behind at Brandy Station than their campsites.

Clark B. Hall
Littleton, Colorado

Preface

This book began with a simple trip to the National Archives to find out what my grandfather had done in the Civil War. My brother and I were adopted as children, and we had little information about our blood father and grandfather, who, appropriately enough, were named Blood. We had a vague impression that our grandfather had been in an Ohio regiment, had served with General William T. Sherman and had lost a leg. We were wrong on all counts.

On March 18, 1864, at Cambridge, Massachusetts, Samuel L. Blood enlisted for three years in the 11th Massachusetts Volunteer Infantry, a part of the Hooker Brigade, a unit of some notoriety. Private Blood was eighteen years one month old. His enlistment certificate indicates he was recruited as a drummer. If that was his role in the army, he did not drum for very long. On May 5, less than two months later, during the battle of the Wilderness, he was struck by a minié ball in the upper right arm, which was subsequently amputated. In trying to understand what happened to my grandfather, I slowly unearthed the strange story of 11th Massachusetts and the Hooker Brigade at a crucial time in their history.

Private Blood joined a military organization racked by controversy and personal animosities. This book is arranged to show the background of this situation and how an army reorganization lit the flames of protest, which led to courts martial for mutiny for the leading dissidents. Next, the unit's controversial performance in the Wilderness and Spotsylvania is examined together with the fate, often bloody and sometimes heroic, of the members of the courts martial board, defendants and witnesses. Finally, the book outlines the subsequent military and postwar careers of the survivors.

Acknowledgments

I wish to thank Michael Musick and others of the staff of the National Archives for their patience and courtesy in dealing with a neophyte Civil War researcher. The library and research staff of the United States Army Military History Institute were also particularly helpful, with special thanks to Dr. Richard Sommers, Michael Winey and other curators of the collection of the Military Order of the Loyal Legion, Massachusetts Commandery. The photographs of MOLLUS, as it is designated, bring the members of the 11th Massachusetts to life. Similar thanks are given to staffs of the Prints and Photographs Division of the Library of Congress and the Still Pictures Branch of National Archives for their help in obtaining photographs. The Library of Congress also provided the drawings of Alfred Waud and Edwin Forbes. My appreciation to John W. Kuhl of Hightown, New Jersey, for the photographs of the men of the 11th New Jersey and to Roger D. Hunt, Rockville, Maryland, for some prints from his extensive collection. My thanks to my newly discovered cousins, Jeane Elizabeth (Blood) Rines and Russell Blood of Saugus, Massachusetts, for the photographs and biographical material relating to Samuel Blood.

The Montana Historical Society was very helpful in obtaining my first extensive leads on Henry N. Blake, and the Harvard University and Harvard Law School libraries supplemented that material. The Blake family also provided additional material and unpublished manuscripts, and my special thanks goes to his great-granddaughter, Patricia Ernsberger of Mill Valley, California, the current family historian. Also thanks to the Historical Society of Pennsylvania for use of the Andrew A. Humphreys Collection and to the Duke University library and the Massachusetts Historical Society for various materials on the 11th Massachusetts. The original drawings of the courts martial and related scenes by Tim Buckett of Ravenna, Ohio, illustrate the story where photos were not available.

My thanks to Donald Pfanz, staff historian of the Fredericksburg and Spotsylvania National Military Park, who reviewed a portion of an early draft and made useful suggestions. I wish to thank John J. Hennessy for his intensive review of a later draft; his comments, suggested text corrections and editorial assistance was most helpful. Thanks also to Brian C. Pohanka, whose expertise on the Army of the Potomac made a review of the final draft necessary and productive.

The task of pulling the manuscripts and photographs into a coherent and readable publication was carried out by the Black Thunder Press in the persons of Katherine Tennery and John Hightower. Thanks also to David Zullo of Olde Soldier Books in Gaithersburg, Maryland, for reading an early draft and suggesting its publication. To Rosemary Hall and Theodore Crolius, my law school roommate and Civil War buff, my thanks for encouragement and editorial assistance.

Finally, I wish to acknowledge the great assistance and encouragement I received from Clark B. Hall. His mastery of everything involving Brandy Station made him an essential resource and his foreword to this work is greatly appreciated.

Frederick B. Amer
Kensington, Maryland
October 15, 1993

Introduction

The mutiny at Brandy Station presents in microcosm the character and actions of the men who served in the United States Army of the Potomac in 1864, the third year of the Civil War. March of 1864 was a time of reorganization. The three year enlistments of the veteran regiments would expire in June. Some of these regiments were transferred from units they had served with great pride and were placed under commanders whose competence and bravery they questioned.

This story reveals officers of truly heroic proportion who believed in their own invulnerability to such a degree as to be detrimental to their physical well-being, men who looked forward to the spring campaign. Most of the enlistees, however, were less sanguine about their futures, and they gave much thought to whether they should reenlist under their new officers at the end of their three year terms. Some were only too aware of their mortality and were sweating out their final days as honorably as possible, and some in this group fell below the minimum norms of performance. In the officer corps, another force was at work. As the war lengthened, the pettiness and vindictiveness of promotion politics increased, accelerated by a winter of relative idleness in camp.

The setting for the mutiny is Brandy Station, Virginia. Ten months had passed since the greatest cavalry battle of the Civil War had been played out on the fields adjoining the tracks of the Orange and Alexandria Railroad. The Fleetwood Hill estate, over which Union and Confederate forces had fought so desperately in June 1863, was now the union headquarters of General George G. Meade's Army of the Potomac. It had been a happy camp during the winter of 1863-1864, and the army had been revitalized. By late March the army numbered about 100,000 men around Brandy Station. The appointment of General Ulysses S. Grant as the commander in chief of all Union forces had

Library of Congress

Brandy Station on the Orange and Alexandria Railroad in Culpeper County, Virginia. Over 100,000 Union troops were stationed around this railhead in the winter of 1863-1864.

Library of Congress

III Corps Headquarters in March 1864 was at the Miller house, Fleetwood Hill, Brandy Station, Virginia.

raised the expectations of the soldiers.

But at this juncture, on March 25, General Meade finalized a reorganization of the army that demoralized some of his most battle-tested veterans. The I Corps and the III Corps were abolished. The latter contained two veteran divisions named after their most distinguished fighting generals, Philip Kearny and Joseph Hooker. The veterans who wore with pride the red (Kearny) and white (Hooker) diamonds, their division insignia, were discontented.

Perhaps the unit most affected by Meade's reorganization, the Hooker Brigade was not only cut from their beloved III Corps, but the brigade itself, in existence since the late summer of 1861, was also broken up. In an effort to keep the brigade intact, the officers requested that the men be held together until their three year enlistments expired. The junior officers of the regiments protested the breakup at a meeting, and five of the so-called ring leaders were arrested and charged with mutiny and other offenses. Four of them were from the 11th Massachusetts Volunteer Infantry.

The focus of the unhappiness of the protesting officers was the appointment of General Joseph B. Carr as their division commander. They considered him sadistic, corrupt, militarily incompetent, and above all cowardly. At the protest meeting, in what they thought were private conversations, some had called him a "cowardly son-of-a-bitch and a rascal." As the Commander of the Hooker Brigade in 1862-1863, his specialty was court martialling the officers of the 11th Massachusetts. When he learned of the meeting, once again he took action.

Carr had a special feud with one of the defendants, Lieutenant Henry N. Blake, an attorney who was the informal but diligent historian of the 11th Massachusetts, and an early and very loud whistle blower. His principal target was Joseph Carr, whom he compared with Caligula and labeled a "starred poltroon," an "ignoramus" and "Celtic vagabond," very strong language in those days.

The bad feeling about the reorganization was exacerbated by some long-standing in-fighting over promotions and personal animosity between two of the bravest regimental commanders of the Hooker Brigade, Colonel William Blaisdell of the 11th Massachusetts and Colonel Robert McAllister of the 11th New Jersey. Blaisdell was a cussing, hard drinking veteran of the Mexican War who was known as "Old Cruelty" for his tough discipline. McAllister, on the other hand, was abstemious and soft-spoken, constant in his attendance at prayer meeting, and continually worried about the spiritual well-being of his troops. Each had been commander of the Hooker Brigade at one time, and Blaisdell, then the incumbent, was removed by the reorganization, an event that apparently brought great joy to the heart of Colonel McAllister.

The courts martial of the five officers were conducted by a board of officers from each of the newly formed II Corps divisions. The proceedings, which went on throughout most of April 1864, are summarized from the original transcripts of the trials.

The aftermath and effect of the trials are assessed by following the II Corps into the battle of the Wilderness and early Spotsylvania, the bloodiest week of the Civil War (May 5-12, 1864). Our focus is on the veteran officers of the 11th Massachusetts, most particularly on Henry Blake, and on the replacement soldiers who joined his company for the spring campaign, including Private Blood. Historical commentaries are generally highly critical of the record of the regiments of the old Hooker Brigade in the Wilderness and at the Salient at Spotsylvania Court House, but with surprisingly little explanation of why these units may have performed below their previous level.

For a broader perspective of the battles in question, the actions of the members of the courts martial board are described as best they can be discerned from available evidence. A surprising number of the participants were not among the living when the smoke of battle had cleared. Among the dead were those whose conduct became legend in the Union Army. It was, indeed, a peculiar "band of brothers" who, with the courts martial barely adjourned, crossed the Rapidan and camped among the skulls at Chancellorsville—a reminder of their previous tragic foray into the Wilderness almost a year earlier to the day.

National Archives

Monument Lot, Washington, first home of the 11th Massachusetts in the Army of the Potomac. The regiment camped here after they arrived by train and marched to the White House (in middle of photograph). The line of trees is along 14th street and the large building is the Treasury Department. The photograph was probably taken from the roof of the old Agriculture Building, with the unfinished Washington Monument just out of sight on the left. The City Canal bordering the lot toward the White House stretched from the Potomac River along what is now Constitution Avenue. Some commentators stated that the 11th was camped on the White House Lot on the far side of the canal, directly in front of the presidential mansion, now called the Ellipse.

Cast of Characters

(page number of photograph noted)

Abbott, Maj. Henry L., 20th Mass.,
courts martial judge *(53)*

Allen, Capt. William C., 11th Mass.,
defense witness *(65)*

Bigelow, Capt. James R., 11th Mass.,
defendant *(55)*

Bingham, Capt. Henry H., II Corps
judge advocate; prosecutor *(51)*

Birney, Gen. David B., 3rd Division,
II Corps, commander *(25)*

Blaisdell, Col. William, 11th Mass.,
commanding officer *(29)*

Blake, Capt. Henry N., 11th Mass.,
defendant and defense attorney *(3)*

Blood, Pvt. Samuel L., 11th Mass.,
replacement soldier *(85)*

Brewster, Col. William R., 73rd N.Y.,
Excelsior Brigade, commander *(52)*

Carr, Lt. James H., 11th N.J., brother of
and aide to Gen. Joseph B. Carr

Carr, Gen. Joseph B., Hooker (4th) Div., II
Corps, commander *(5)*

DuPaget, Lt. Alfred, 11th N.J.,
prosecution witness

Forrest, Lt. George, 11th Mass.,
defendant *(77)*

French, Gen. William H., III Corps
commander, 1863-1864 *(28)*

Grover, Gen. Cuvier, Hooker Brigade
commander, 1862 *(2)*

Hancock, Gen. Winfield Scott, II Corps
commander *(47)*

Hamilton, Capt. James, 105th Pa.,
courts martial judge

Hays, Gen. Alexander, brig. commander, 3rd
Div., II Corps; courts martial judge *(51)*

Hooker, Gen. Joseph, organized the 1st
Brig., 2nd Div., III Corps in 1861 *(2)*

Humphreys, Gen. Andrew A., Hooker Div.
commander, 1863; Chief of Staff,
Army of Potomac *(34, 175)*

Lombard, Capt. Richard, 16th Mass.,
defense witness

Marston, Gen. Gilman, 2nd N.H.,
commander *(7)*

McAllister, Col. Robert, 11th N.J.,
commander *(29)*

McAllister, Capt. William, 140th Pa.,
courts martial judge

McLaughlen, Col. Napoleon Bonaparte,
1st Mass., commander *(45)*

Merriam, Col. Waldo, 16th Mass.,
commander; courts martial judge *(52)*

Morehouse, Act. Lt. Benjamin, 11th N.J.,
prosecution witness *(58)*

Mott, Gen. Gershom, Hooker (4th) Division,
II Corps, commander *(48)*

Munroe, Capt. William, 11th Mass.,
defense witness *(65)*

Nelson, Maj. Peter, 66th N.Y.,
courts martial judge

Prince, Gen. Henry, Hooker (2nd) Div.,
III Corps, commander *(28)*

Rivers, Capt. Charles C., 11th Mass.,
defense witness *(65)*

Rockhill, Act. Lt. William S., 11th N.J.,
prosecution witness *(58)*

Schoonover, Lt. Col. John, 11th N.J.,
deputy commander; hostile defense
witness *(48)*

Sleeper, Capt. Samuel T., 11th N.J.,
prosecution witness *(58)*

Smith, Lt. John H., 11th N.J.,
defense witness

Smith, Capt. Walter N., 11th Mass.,
defendant *(73)*

Sowter, Capt. John, 11th N.J.,
defense witness *(74)*

Starbird, Capt. Isaac, 19th Maine,
courts martial judge *(53)*

Teaffle, Adj. Lt. William, 11th Mass.,
defense witness (65)

Thomas, Capt. Edward C., 26th Pa.,
defendant

Tripp, Lt. Col. Porter D., 11th Mass.,
deputy commander *(23)*

Walker, Lt. Col. Francis, II Corps Asst. Adj.
Gen.; signed courts martial charges *(47)*

White, Capt. Rufus, 11th Mass.,
defense witness *(65)*

I. The Hooker Brigade

The Veterans

In mid March of 1864 the 11th Massachusetts had been in the Army of the Potomac since early June 1861, just short of three years. The enlistments of its veterans would expire within three months. According to Gustavus B. Hutchinson, a sergeant in Company D, the 11th was among the first regiments to respond to President Abraham Lincoln's call for volunteers. On their way to Washington, D.C., they marched through cheering crowds in Boston, their officers were entertained at the Astor House in New York, and the regiment was greeted personally by President Lincoln in Washington. Their camp was on the Monument Grounds, just across from the Treasury Department and the White House.(1)

But the glory days of campground soldiering were short lived, and by July they had been blooded and bowed in the first battle of Bull Run and the rout that followed. After Bull Run the 11th and three other regiments were rejuvenated by a newly appointed brigade commander, Brigadier General Joseph Hooker, and went on to serve with distinction in some of the bloodiest fighting on the Peninsula, at Second Bull Run, Chancellorsville and Gettysburg. At Gettysburg, and up until the reorganization, the Hooker Brigade included three of the oldest Massachusetts regiments—the 1st, 11th, and 16th—and the 26th Pennsylvania, whose service together dated back to the Peninsular Campaign. The 11th New Jersey joined the brigade at Fredericksburg in late 1862, when General Joseph Bradford Carr became the brigade commander. The 84th Pennsylvania was added just before the battle at Gettysburg.

Prior to General George G. Meade's reorganization of the Union forces in 1864, the 11th Massachusetts was in the Second Division of the III Corps; it had been Hooker's division through Second Bull Run. The memories of their

Library of Congress
"Fighting Joe" Hooker organized and trained the brigade after First Bull Run, at the Bladensburg dueling grounds outside Washington, D.C.

USAMHI
Cuvier Grover commanded the Hooker Brigade on the Peninsula and led a bayonet charge at Second Bull Run.

brave brigade commander, General Cuvier Grover, and earlier division commanders, Daniel Sickles at Fredericksburg and Hiram Berry, who was killed at Chancellorsville, were much on their minds. Their recent leaders were found wanting in comparison.

At the time of reorganization, the officer with the lowest approval rating from the 11th Massachusetts was General Carr. The man who would report his deficiencies to the world was First Lieutenant Henry N. Blake. Feuds among colonels are relatively common, but when a lieutenant takes on a brigadier general it is usually no contest. Henry Blake was, however, a worthy opponent for General Carr and one not to be underestimated.

2

Henry N. Blake—
Proper Bostonian

Blake was from Dorchester, Massachusetts, had graduated from Harvard Law School in 1858, and had practiced law briefly in Boston before the war. He supported Abraham Lincoln in the election of 1860 and tramped many miles with the Lincoln Wide-Awakes, one of the more colorful elements of the campaign. The Wide-Awakes were uniformly garbed in cap and cape and carried a lamp on a staff as they paraded through the streets and aroused momentary enthusiasm in eastern Massachusetts.(2)

MOLLUS-USAMHI
Captain Henry N. Blake, Company K, 11th Massachusetts, was an early and fearless whistle-blower.

After the President's call for volunteers, Blake enlisted as a private in Company K of the 11th Massachusetts, the Dorchester Company, concealing his glasses to get through the physical. He was slightly wounded at First Bull Run, and by the time of the Peninsula Campaign in early 1862 he was first sergeant of his company. On the basis of his performance at the battle of Williamsburg, he was commissioned a second lieutenant for brave and meritorious conduct.

When Company K's commander, Captain Benjamin Stone, was mortally wounded at Second Bull Run, Blake replaced First Lieutenant William Munroe, who moved up to captain. Lieutenant Blake acted as the regiment's lawyer, and on his own initiative became their historian and general all-purpose scribe. His intrepid note-taking between May 1861 and May 1864, when he was mustered out, resulted in a book, *Three Years in the Army of the Potomac,* published in April 1865.

Colonel Robert McAllister, commander of the 11th New Jersey, in one of his letters described Blake as:

a lawyer [who] has some smartness about him. But having a dislike for General Carr because the General had him court martialled, he has never forgiven him and has been doing all he could against Carr's confirmation in Washington.(3)

The appraisal is basically correct, but other than this letter, there is little evidence that Blake had actively opposed Carr's confirmation in Washington. Blake did have access to Senator Henry Wilson of Massachusetts, chairman of the Senate Committee on Military Affairs, and when asked in early 1864 had communicated his observations of General William H. French, his corps commander. At that time, however, Carr was the commander of another division. Such an action would have been a little out of character for Blake, who wrote in strong terms against political meddling in army affairs, but it was very true that Blake did not like General Carr.

A review of his book in the *Army and Navy Journal* in May 1865 caught the essence of Blake:

It is the boldest and bitterest stricture on military operations as yet evoked by this war—a spoonful of fresh horseradish, quite a relish in its peculiarity. If sustained by evidence, it will prove an important source of information for writers upon the operations of the Army of the Potomac. Without intending to express any decision upon its historical merits at the present time, or upon its errors—it is clearly and agreeably written, and well worthy of examination, if only as a curiosity in the military literature of the war. The author, we are told, is a brave and capable man, keen, observant, chiefly celebrated in the army as a chess player, and judging from his career in arms, irrespective of that with his pen, one of the most fearless who has ever undertaken to expose what he deemed abuses and defects in military movements, administrations and men.(4)

Joseph B. Carr—
Brave Trojan General or Starred Poltroon?

Joseph Bradford Carr was born in 1828 to Irish parents in Albany, New York, and later moved to Troy, New York. When the war began, he was in the tobacco business and a colonel in the state militia. He recruited the 2nd New York regiment, was commissioned its colonel in May 1861, and led it at Big

Bethel, Virginia, one of the first battles of the Civil War, on June 10, 1861. He commanded the Third Brigade of Hooker's Division on the Peninsula and was promoted to brigadier general of United States volunteers in September 1862.

A eulogy written after Carr's death in 1865 observed that "a profane or objectionable word was never heard from his mouth."(5)

In letters written by General Robert McAllister, Carr is portrayed in a friendly, if not saintly fashion. McAllister's editor concludes from the letters that Carr was "an unpretentious officer who preferred to do his duty fully and quietly."(6)

The Troy *Daily Times,* Carr's hometown newspaper, lauded the general in an article dated June 15, 1865.

USAMHI

Gen. Joseph B. Carr, Commander of the Hooker Brigade (1862-63), Third Division, III Corps (1863-64), and Fourth Division, II Corps (Mar-Apr 1864)

A most creditable and brilliant record has General Carr made during the war. The tributes of General Hooker, General Meade and General [Andrew Atkinson] Humphreys are evidences of his heroism, and proof of his abilities and success as a commanding officer. We realize peculiar pleasures, in common with all our citizens, in knowing that Troy has had so gallant a representative in the tremendous work of crushing the rebellion. And the satisfaction is heightened from the fact that Gen. Carr has won honorable distinction by real work, by gallant performance on the field of battle, by the exhibition of cool courage and superior abilities amid the dangers of bloody contests. Our Trojan General, without adventitious aids, never appealing to political power to secure advancement—rising from the ranks of the working people, and by diligence in study, zealous labor in his vocation, natural aptitude for his profession, and fervent patriotism to stimulate his endeavors—has secured the plaudits of our ablest commanders, and the honorable recognition of the Government.(7)

Not every report on Carr was so glowing. One of the defendant officers at the Brandy Station courts martial detailed in later chapters called Carr a cowardly son-of-a-bitch and a rascal. Unfortunately for him, the accuracy of his statement was ruled irrelevant and not admissable at his trial, although it might have been in another trial, if General Carr had sued Captain Blake for libel. Presumably to avoid litigation, although he denies it, Blake never refers by name to Carr in his book. But the people he was primarily writing for—his fellow soldiers—knew exactly who he was talking about. Blake's general appraisal of Carr does not equivocate. He wrote that General Meade, in appointing General Carr to division commander instead of General Alexander Hays, "displayed a censurable ignorance, or lack of judgment." Of Carr he wrote:

[O]ne division was almost demoralized by the appointment of a notorious coward, knave, and ignoramus to the command. A general who
always deserted his brigade whenever the trials of battle demanded his
presence; who never discharged the numberless accounts of the sutlers
and commissaries for food, rations, and liquors which he consumed; who
employed escaped negroes as servants, and defrauded them of their just
compensation; who displayed a profound ignorance upon every subject,
which made him the butt of ridicule for soldiers of all ranks, from the
highest to the lowest.(8)

Blake outlines in some detail the problems he has with General Carr's command and fighting characteristics. Carr as commander of the Hooker Brigade replaced General Cuvier Grover, a front-line soldier who had led the unit in a bayonet charge at the railroad embankment at Second Bull Run. Blake wrote that during the spring of 1863, when the brigade was out of its camp at Falmouth and guarding the right of the army on the Rappahannock,

The brigade . . . was usually commanded by a field-officer, while the
general enjoyed the safety and comfort of his tent in camp. Upon one
occasion, when [Confederate General James E. B. "Jeb"] Stuart crossed
the stream and an attack was anticipated, a brigadier boldly ordered a
colonel, who had arrived from his home which he had visited with leave,

to proceed at once to the front, and take charge of his troops. The conduct of this starred poltroon was in striking contrast with that of commanders like Generals [Philip] Kearny, Hooker and Grover.(9)

At about this same time at Falmouth, General Carr was having trouble with the United States Senate, which had not confirmed his appointment as brigadier general. Colonel Gilman Marston, who organized and commanded the 2nd New Hampshire, had developed a dislike for Carr, and it was rumored that he would take over the Hooker Brigade. On March 30, 1863, General McAllister wrote his wife that General Carr was about to leave the brigade because he had an enemy who was working against him.

Col. Marston was also a member of Congress. While acting as Colonel here, he took offense at

Library of Congress
General Gilman Marston, who commanded the 2nd New Hampshire (1861-63); Point Lookout Prison Camp (1863-64); and the First Brigade, First Division, XVIII Corps (1864), was an early critic of Joseph Carr.

Carr because Carr would not let him do as he pleased—i.e. be away from his regiment. And it is said that Marston swore that he could make and break Generals. So, you see, he has been working with the President and War Department, and has prevented Carr's confirmation. Col. Marston was also nominated for Brigadier General. I cannot say whether he was confirmed or not but I rather think he was. We all now fear that now he will be placed over us in Carr's place. All the officers in this Brigade are friendly to Gen. Carr and, of course, are very opposed to Col. Marston. Carr is a splendid man, a good General, and his heart is in the work. He is a *grate Union Man,* (with or without the nigger) and a warm supporter of the administration. He wished to stay in the Army to do or die for his country. A great friend of the Volunteers and opposed to Regulars, he is

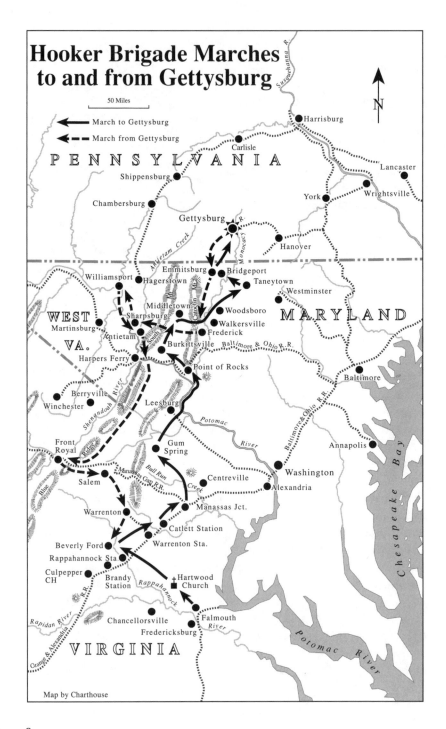

Hooker Brigade Marches to and from Gettysburg

50 Miles

→ March to Gettysburg

◄- - - March from Gettysburg

N

PENNSYLVANIA

Harrisburg

Carlisle

Lancaster

Shippensburg

Chambersburg

York

Wrightsville

Gettysburg

Hanover

Antietam Creek

Williamsport   Emmitsburg   Bridgeport

Hagerstown

Taneytown

Westminster

Middletown   Woodsboro

MARYLAND

Sharpsburg

Walkersville

WEST

Martinsburg

Antietam   Frederick

Burkittsville   *Baltimore & Ohio R.R.*

VA.

Harpers Ferry

Point of Rocks

Baltimore

Berryville

Winchester   Leesburg

Potomac

Shenandoah River

River

Front Royal   Gum Spring

Annapolis

Manassas Gap R.R.   Centreville

Washington

Salem   *Bull Run Creek*

Alexandria

Warrenton   Manassas Jct.

Catlett Station

Beverly Ford   Warrenton Sta.

Rappahannock Sta.

Culpepper CH   Brandy Station

Hartwood Church

Rappahannock River

Rapidan River

Chancellorsville   Falmouth

Fredericksburg   *River*

VIRGINIA

Potomac River

Chesapeake Bay

Orange & Alexandria R.R.

Map by Charthouse

8

a very kind and sociable man—ever ready to do an act of kindness to those who needed it.(10)

A few days later, however, General Marston was assigned to command the new prison camp at Point Lookout , and Carr remained with the Hooker Brigade.

The March to Gettysburg

The march to Gettysburg in June of 1863 revealed what Blake considered to be the sadistic side of General Carr:

Caligula and other monsters of antiquity never displayed a more diabolical spirit than certain generals in the corps, who murdered the unfortunate soldiers that were compelled to obey their orders, by exhausting their strength, and needlessly exposing them to rays of the sun, which through their cruelty, became as deadly as minié balls. There is not more than one in ten officers of high rank that understands the proper mode of moving a division; fatigue that so often results is caused, not merely traveling a large number of miles, but by the omission to halt them at regular intervals after marching short distances. Mounted upon their horses, unencumbered by rations, or clothing, and usually carrying a small flask and a light sword, it was a pastime for the subordinate generals and their staffs to ride or race from town to town, and issue stringent orders to court-martial the weary men for what they termed straggling.(11)

On June 11, just over a month after Chancellorsville, the officers of the 11th Massachusetts were playing baseball when an order came to break camp at Falmouth because Confederate General Robert E. Lee was on the march north. The III Corps was ordered to guard the crossings of the Rappahannock from Kelly's Ford to Beverly Ford.(12) The 11th moved out within an hour, and Blake noted that Carr, "the general commanding the brigade, pushed forward the troops in a most unmerciful manner, and great joy was manifested when they bivouacked near Hartwood Church."(13) Blake wrote that the next day the division marched from 5:20 A.M., until 9:20 P.M., upon one of the warmest days of the month, and always designedly halted in the open fields, while a general enjoyed the comfort of the extensive forests in the vicinity, and, with the hearts of demons, laughed and uttered jokes about the soldiers who were dying or writhing in the agonies of sun-stroke. Some surgeons and regimental commanders remonstrated against this inhuman conduct, and told a general that it was killing the men; but he sneeringly remarked, "I want to tire them out, so they can't run away;" "If I can stand it, the men can;" or "The sun will dry their shirts, if they are wet with perspiration." I speak with emphatic language, for I recall the forms of prostrate heroes who had escaped the bullet, the shell, and the "fiery darts" of the foe in scenes of combat, and fell fainting by the roadside, to die, or linger in pain from which they never recovered. Thousands of throats were sometimes screaming, "Halt, halt!" and there were universal cries, "Kick him out of the house!" "I hope the rebels will kill him!" "Shoot the scoundrel!" interlaced with the most profane oaths ever uttered, when the command passed by the mansion selected for headquarters. Some men seized the general's servant, who had walked a long distance to procure cool water, and spitefully confiscated the property. Less than one-third of the Division bivouacked at Beverly Ford; and the stream of soldiers that had forced by the foregoing causes to leave the ranks were continually flowing into the regiment during the night.(14)

Chaplain Warren H. Cudworth of the 1st Massachusetts wrote of the march to Beverly Ford, "nearly thirty miles were traversed at a rapid pace, through clouds of dust in some places so dense, that vision was impossible beyond a few yards; and a large number of men fell out by the wayside, utterly overcome by heat and fatigue."(15)

Captain A. W. Bartlett, the historian of the 12th New Hampshire, wrote that this "was one of the hardest marches ever made by the Army of the Potomac."(16)

The Hooker Brigade remained in the Beverly Ford area until the evening of June 14, when the cavalry was assigned to patrol duties on the Rappahannock. The brigade marched all night and arrived at Catlett Station at 7:10 A.M. At 8:40 A.M., according to Blake, it moved again and did not halt until it was near Warrenton Station at midnight. The brigade followed a train of wagons that tore up the dirt road and made the march uneven and difficult. Blake described Carr's regimen for the march:

The soldiers were forced to halt in the fields, without any shelter from the sun; and those who were overcome by the severe fatigue which always follows a movement in the night, and fell asleep, awoke to suffer from intense faintness and pain, which disabled them for years. . . . Many a soldier uttered the wish that he might be permitted to serve out the remaining months of his term of service in some prison, or be changed into the general's horse, when he beheld that officer with his staff and their steeds reposing in the vast forest from which they were exclused. The region was unusually dry; and the men, urged by necessity, slackened to a slight extent their thirst by extracting the moisture from the lumps of damp earth. Thousands were exhausted, and sought the woods to recover their strength; but a general issued orders to the provost-guard to set the dry leaves on fire, and thus drive the members of his force into the cleared tracts of land, and clouds of smoke rolled upwards in the rear of the column. The combined heat of the rays of the sun and burning forest was unendurable; the breath seemed to be a flame; and less than one-fourth of the division rested at the bivouac.(17)

Chaplain Cudworth also wrote of the march to Warrenton Junction:

The men were kept marching all night, by a circuitous route, and arrived at their destination at eight o'clock the next morning. . . . The weather at this time was oppressively warm, the roads as dry as ashes, and water scarce, which combined to produce an unprecedented amount of suffering among the troops. The daily marches were usually long, and made at an unusually rapid pace; so that the roads were lined with stragglers representing almost every regiment, some of whom had been sun-struck, and were completely broken down. To add to the discomforts ordinarily experienced, the woods and fields had been set on fire, intentionally or otherwise, which filled the atmosphere with smoke and cinders, compelling the soldiers to bivouac upon the open plains.(18)

This march was still vivid in the memory of a survivor of the 26th Pennsylvania who spoke at the dedication of the Pennsylvania memorial at Gettysburg in September 1889. Thomas V. Cooper declared, "Our march from

Bealeton to Manassas is remembered as one of the hottest, many of the division and corps falling from sunstroke, so that when night came the losses, if they had been compiled, would have held comparison with a battle."(19)

Captain Bartlett reported, "This was a harder march even than that of the 12th [of June], for the men were not in so good a condition to make it, their feet being so badly blistered that some left blood in their tracks through the hot sand."(20)

On June 16 the brigade crossed Bull Run, reached Centerville on the 17th, on the 19th arrived at Gum Springs [now Arcola] and the next six days were spent there supporting the pickets. Gum Springs, noted for its purity since General Braddock's time, was used by General Carr in a manner that did not instill love of his person among his troops. Blake wrote that armed guards prevented "the soldiers from enjoying the priceless liquid without a permit in writing from the general. [The] drivers, who daily renewed the water in the kegs which are attached to the ambulances to convey a fresh supply for the weary, the sick, or other wounded, were pushed aside at the point of the bayonet, and directed to a turbulent run in which horses and mules were standing or walking, and the men were washing their persons and clothes." He recorded the words of one soldier, accompanied by oaths, that "I hope General —— will be shot, and live just long enough for me to pour my keg-full of this gravel down his throat!"(21)

From Gum Springs another march of major proportions was undertaken, an 18 hour affair to the mouth of the Monocacy River in Maryland, with its final phase a night march on the C&O canal tow-path in driving rain. All accounts are that the soldiers slipped, slid and finally stopped dead in their tracks late at night, spread out along the canal wherever they could find a level space.

Blake stated that generals Humphreys and Carr "dashed ahead of the column to secure a pleasant repose for the night." When the commander of the 11th Massachusetts finally stopped the regiment without orders, Blake noted that "only eighteen muskets were stacked in a line that should have had 324 arms." Blake wrote that "a general greeted the appearance of the remnant of his command in the morning with hearty laughter, and uttered many gibes concerning their weakness, and the condition of those who were without shoes, and bound handkerchiefs and towels around their feet, or wore two or three pairs of socks;" and made this remark about the regiment as it filed by him: "What regiment is that? Bring them here, and we will pray for them."(22)

Cudworth also remembered the march. He wrote that

for length, severity, and discomfort, [it] exceeded anything the army ever had been through before. . . . [On the towpath] there was no place to rest, with any comfort; and therefore the march was kept up, at a quick pace, until one o'clock, A.M. The consequence was that whole regiments fell out of line, and stayed until morning on the narrow strip of land between the river and the canal; while, of other regiments, not more than one man in ten attempted to push through with the head of the column. Three hundred and sixty men belonging to the 1st left Gum Spring in the morning; but only forty laid down in the rains, seventeen hours after, on the banks of the Monocacy. The rest had given out.(23)

Private Cooper of the 26th Pennsylvania recalled the infamous march in his 1889 speech:

No man who participated in that march can ever forget the driving rain, the slippery and narrow pathway, with water to the right of us, water to the left of us, water above, water below—without opportunity to halt, or rest, or eat or drink, until the late hours of the night found us at our destination.(24)

The tow-path march made a division-wide impression. Martin A. Haynes, the historian of the 2nd New Hampshire, pointed out that there were two routes,

[a] highway broad and direct, affording excellent passage for troops, upon the other the tow-path, a narrow bank between the river and canal. Upon the latter road the division was led, and the general congratulated himself that he had got his machines upon a track where there was no opportunity for straggling. His stout horse lead off a slashing gait, and the column followed after. . . . Horse-flesh won. One by one, and squad by squad the exhausted men sank upon the ground and refused to go farther, until the little plots of land which occasionally intervened upon the river side were covered with the stragglers. Commanders of regiments were left without the colors and almost without men, and finally some of them followed the example of the men, until the general had arrived at his goal he had hardly men enough to form a respectable headquarters guard.(25)

Blake wrote that after these grueling marches, "the attention of an officer of high rank was called to the large number of deaths and casualties from sunstroke and exhaustion in a certain command; and the generals were compelled to halt a few minutes in every hour; and long distances were thus marched with ease."(26)

General David B. Birney, the acting corps commander in the absence of General Daniel Sickles, was probably the "officer of high rank." On June 17 he issued a circular which stated in part that

officers leading the column will, whenever practicable, lead it through fields, avoiding the dusty roads, and will halt sufficiently often to keep it well closed. . . . Officers are charged with the responsibility of keeping their commands together, and it is hoped that the emergency will interest all in making every possible effort to expedite the column.(27)

The Confederates had learned this marching technique early in the war from General Thomas J. "Stonewall" Jackson, who had issued a circular on the subject to his corps two weeks before his famous march around the Union army at Chancellorsville.(28) It is interesting to note that after the tow-path mud march, there are many notations of two hour breaks and stops for supper in General Carr's reports.(29)

The march of the brigade in northern Maryland was relatively easy and Lieutenant Blake recorded an example of General Carr "quietly doing his duty" and the response of the soldiers:

One general in the division, well known for his cowardice, marched through the populous districts with much ostentation at the head of his brigade, and shouted orders in a pompous tone of authority to attract the notice of the crowd; while the soldiers were saying, "It is perfectly safe to be in front now;" "There won't be any fighting while he leads the brigade," and similar sentences. This officer had taught dancing schools of a low character before the war; and the members of some companies would "call off" the various changes,—"Right and left," "All promenade to the bar," whenever he rode by them, for the purpose of insulting him.(30)

The Second Division's final approach to Gettysburg had its humorous moments. General Humphreys had joined the march when it reached Marsh

National Archives
The Black Horse Tavern, site of General Andrew Humphreys' unexpected encounter with the Confederates, in a photograph taken long after the war.

Run, just outside of Gettysburg. Humphreys later claimed that a staff officer of General Sickles, Lieutenant Colonel Julius Hayden, who was sent out to usher him in, was "positive" that he should come in by the Black Horse Tavern on the Fairfield-Gettysburg road. Humphreys wrote that he rode at the head of the column, without an advance guard.(31)

Carr wrote in his report, however, that "Hayden, who had been in advance with the guides, soon after rode up to General Humphreys, and stated that we were but 200 yards from the enemy's pickets."(32) General Humphreys checked with the proprietor of the tavern, who verified the presence of the Confederates. The Second Division then executed a very quick about face.

Blake described the incident:

A negro, who was greatly excited and scarcely able to speak because he knew that the soldiers were marching in the wrong direction earnestly said to a general, "The road is full of 'em,—heaps of rebels!" but that officer avowed his leading principle to be, "Never believe a nigger," and the column pressed on. . . . [The] infantry was forced to wade through Marsh Creek several hundred yards, and not allowed to pass over the covered bridge; while a general and his staff sat upon their horses, and amused themselves by laughing at those on foot in the stream. A citizen remarked, "If you go on, you will have a fight in the night," and one of the rebel pickets who was searching for water found himself a prisoner in the hands of the advance guard at ten P.M. The regiments were at once halted in the road, and ordered not to talk or light matches; while the mounted officers . . . promptly retired to the rear (now the front); and the three long miles which had been uselessly traveled were retraced in silence. Willoughby's Run was forded; the vedettes of the cavalry were passed within a short distance of the blazing camp-fires of the enemy; and the division joined the III Corps, and bivouacked upon the plains of Gettysburg at half-past two, A.M., on July 2.(33)

General Carr at Gettysburg

Lieutenant Blake reports on Carr's performance at Gettysburg as an example of his overall military ability. When General Sickles moved the III Corps forward on the second day, Carr's brigade was on the right of the Union line on the Emmitsburg Road. The 11th Massachusetts was at the Peter Rogers farm house. The first Confederate attacks were concentrated on the Union left. When the Confederates finally attacked the right, the line on the left was already in deep trouble. The 11th Massachusetts supported John C. Turnbull's battery, on its left, which had been effectively raking the attacking Confederates with canister. Blake wrote that "all thought that the repulse might be decisive" but

before the regiment could deliver its volley, the companies about-faced in pursuance of the orders of some stupid general, and executed a right half-wheel under a severe fire, with as much regularity as if they had been upon parade, and thus abandoned the advantages of the strong line of defense. The "stars and bars" of treason were visible when the infantry could not be seen; and the column which had been shattered by the battery appeared in front, and began to shoot the gunners, who performed their duty with the utmost fidelity, and retired at last to escape the capture which seemed unavoidable. . . . The soldiers were constantly loading and aiming their rifles at the breasts of the members of the [Confederate] regiment, [when] orders were duly transmitted from a blockhead, termed upon the muster-roll a brigadier-general, not to discharge a musket,

National Archives
Josephine Miller, granddaughter of the Rogers family, was baking bread for a few Massachusetts soldiers who had liberated some flour from Gen. Sickle's commissary. Blake noted that only after a Confederate cannon ball knocked out her stove was she finally convinced to take cover in the cellar. She was the only woman member of the III Corps Veterans Association. She is shown here with her stove at a reunion, probably in the late 1880s.

because they "would fire upon their own men"; and the enemy was enabled in this way to cut down the ranks, and diminish the effect of the first volley.(34)

At this point Blake, with tongue in cheek, excused his "block head" commander.

Candor compels me to admit that this mistake was excusable upon this ground, that the officer from his standpoint, which was far in the rear, could not distinguish one line of battle from the other.(35)

Blake then reported that the situation was deteriorating.

The right of the brigade was not within the supporting distance of the II Corps: the left of the division had been forced to fall back, so that the troops were subjected in certain positions to volleys from three distinct points, and the men slowly retreated, foot by foot; while thousands, pierced by the deadly minié balls, or torn asunder by the explosion of the infernal shell-bullet, fell, and saturated the plain with their blood.(36)

Apparently the fighting was getting close to General Carr when Blake recorded the following.

As soon as the bullets began to whistle, a general said to the orderly who carried the colors of his brigade, which he supposed would attract notice and draw the fire of the enemy upon him, "Take away that flag. Go to the rear with that flag;" and the person who obeyed this direction remarked in stating it, "Faith, an' I was as willin' to run with it to the rear as he was to have me."(37)

Lieutenant Blake noted that this might have had a disastrous effect if the troops had been new, "but they were veterans, and the shameful misconduct of the officers who commanded them did not affect their constancy or firmness."](38)

In Blake's view it was never necessary for the troops to issue the call, "Carr to the rear." But contrast Blake's description with that of the Troy *Daily Times* in describing Carr's actions at Gettysburg:

In the midst of the raging conflict when the iron hail was flying thick and fast, he was reminded by one of his aides of his danger; but steadily he moved along in front of his battalions, securing the confidence of his soldiers, and receiving plaudits from the commanders around him. His valuable horse, presented by admiring friends in Troy, fell pierced with five bullets, and in the fall injured the General's leg. Though barely able to stand, lame and exhausted as he was, he disregarded the entreaties of his staff officers to retire from the field, and, mounting another horse, continued to direct the movements of his brigade.(39)

If General Carr actually rode in front of the 11th Massachusetts at Gettysburg, even Blake would agree that he was indeed a very brave man.

The retreat of the brigade was orderly, and the Confederates were feeling some of the weight of their losses. The II Corps launched a counter attack on their left flank and by sunset the Hooker Brigade had joined in. Blake wrote:

MOLLUS-USAMHI

Union dead along the Emmitsburg Road, Gettysburg.

In obedience to a universal cry among the soldiers, "Charge on Them!" "Take our old ground!" the fragment of the brigade, with the colors of five regiments unfurled within the distance of one hundred feet, in the absence of its general, and against the orders of Gen. Humphreys, the division commander, who vainly shouted, "Halt, Halt!—stop those men!" pursued the enemy half of a mile, captured several hundred prisoners, retook cannon that had been left upon the field, and assisted to achieve a conclusive success. Those who suffered from fatigue in retreating before a victorious foe until they could barely move recovered their strength when the circumstances were reversed, and they gladly ran to overtake the defeated force.(40)

But the frolic ended, Blake wrote, with the authorities on their trail.

One of the staff arrived, and stated that a brigadier-general had decided to establish a new line of battle about a mile in the rear, but was unable to find his regiments, and delivered an order for ranks to return at once to that point. The men were very indignant, because they wished to enjoy that rest which is so precious to every soldier—a sleep upon the field which they had won by their bravery; and an officer said, "Tell the

19

general, that, if he will come to the front, he will find his commands with their colors; and, if he was not such a d—d coward, he would be here with them."(41)

Eventually the regiments returned to General Carr's line. Blake summed up the losses for the day:

More than one-half the division was disabled; eight color-bearers of the regiment fell while the flag passed from one to another, and was never lowered; and the company to which I was assigned [Co. K], which had thirty muskets at the commencement of the action, lost nineteen men by the bullet, seven of whom died of their injuries.(42)

MOLLUS-USAMHI
Monument to the 11th Massachusetts at Gettysburg. The monument today is without its sword, due to vandalism.

An article in the Dorchester (Mass.) *Beacon* of July 22, 1899 stated that "Company K lost more men in this engagement than any other organization of the field. Every man was hit or injured in some way, or taken prisoner. Of the 31 men who started in, only five, besides the officers, were fit for duty after the battle. Corporal. E. F. Gleason was wounded twice, and Corporal Martin Stone was killed, as were six others—one fourth of the whole company."

On the third day at Gettysburg, the III Corps went into the reserve on Cemetery Ridge. Other than being under the massive artillery barrage that preceded Pickett's charge, they were not otherwise engaged. Blake observed Carr on that relatively quiet day:

The most amusing spectacle that I witnessed was a frightened brigadier-general, who sat in a wheelbarrow near a fence, dodged missiles which did not come near him, and seemed to shrink to about one-third of his natural size.(43)

Chasing Lee Into Virginia

B lake's description of the exit from Gettysburg after the battle indicated the further deterioration of the Blake-Carr relationship. As the III Corps followed Lee along the eastern base of the Blue Ridge, moving toward Manassas Gap, Blake wrote that

> a general gratified his tyrannical disposition by sending the pioneers in advance of his command to cut down and destroy all "foot bridges" so that the men would be compelled to wade through the numerous streams that intersected the road, and endure the suffering which always followed, while the scene highly entertained him and his staff. A woman in a village complained that a certain general treated her worse than the privates of his brigade; by cheating ignorant people in making change, or obtaining baskets and dishes by promising to return them when their contents had been consumed, were laughed over as splendid jokes at his headquarters.(44)

Blake's final report on Carr's military bearing was written on July 24, when the brigade was pursuing the rear guard of Lee's Confederate army around Front Royal. Blake noted that when a rebel battery threw three shells at the lead column,

> the brigade at once filed to the right of the road, formed a line of battle in the woods, and waited for further orders. A small hill which rose abruptly in front interfered with the view in that direction; and, after the skirmishers had advanced, aides and others officers boldly rode upon the crest and examined the ground; while a general who showed base cowardice upon every occasion of danger timidly stood upon the slope,

21

so that his eyes could barely see the position, and repeating his ignoble conduct at Gettysburg, told the color bearer of his brigade to "go to the rear." When the troops were ordered to move forward, this general was attacked by a disease which might be truly termed a case of indisposition; and the command devolved upon a lieutenant-colonel, who shouted orders in a loud voice which might have been heard by the entire force of both armies. The first height was passed without opposition; and the men expected to receive a volley from the thick woods that crowned another hill which was beyond it, until skirmishers reported that the rebel cavalry were racing through the streets of Front Royal. When those in the rear learned this fact, the general, whose recovery had been as sudden as his illness, resumed his place amidst a thousand half-suppressed mutters and curses about the "coward" and "playing sick."(45)

On the march from Piedmont to Manassas Gap, there was an incident involving Carr and Blake that might be dubbed the battle of the Brook. Blake wrote about it:

While the column was fording a broad stream that was knee-deep, a general (for whom, viewed as an officer or man, no one entertained any respect) vainly ordered the soldiers of his command to march in another place, and shouting to an officer, he pointed to a hole in the road where the water was four feet in depth, "Lieutenant, you go through there." No delay would have been allowed; and this lieutenant, knowing that the rations and ammunition of his company would be ruined if this useless order was obeyed, did not deviate from his course, and by refusing to walk through cold, soon found himself in hot water, and placed in arrest.(46)

The lieutenant, of course, was none other than Henry Blake. His court martial was held near Warrenton on July 30, 1863, with General Carr as the only government witness.(47) Blake was his own attorney, and was able to cross examine his brigade commander. The charge was that Blake, upon being asked by the general whether he had heard his order to march his company through the stream, answered in "an insolent tone and manner, 'Yes, I hear you,' but still failed to obey." This, in the words of the charge, was "in the presence and hearing of the enlisted men of his Regiment setting them an example of insubordination calculated to subvert good order and military discipline." Carr said he asked Blake four times if he heard the order and on the fourth made his affirmative reply "in a very insulting manner."

Blake based his defense on two issues: whether his answer was insolent and the depth of the stream. On cross examination, General Carr stated that in his opinion "the deepest portion of that stream might have been from six inches to one foot deep. Maybe more." Defense attorney Blake, never to be outgunned in the number of witnesses, then had two officers from the 11th Massachusetts, including his company commander, Captain Munroe, say the water was "two to two and one half feet" and "waist deep."

MOLLUS-USAMHI

Lt. Col. Porter D. Tripp, Acting Commander of the 11th Massachusetts during the summer of 1863 when Col. Blaisdell was absent due to illness, presided at Henry Blake's first court martial.

As to the charge of insolence, Blake asked Carr on cross examination whether he was acquainted with him or familiar with his tone or manners. The general answered in the negative. Blake's final defense witness was a Sergeant Stone from the company behind him on the line of march. Blake asked Stone, "Was my manner insolent?" The sergeant testified that Blake "answered in a gentlemanly manner." The court found Blake guilty of disobeying orders but not "in an insolent tone and manner," and he was sentenced to "be privately reprimanded by the General Commanding the Brigade."

Blake wrote that "although the general committed perjury, . . . witnesses of inferior rank, but superior courage, honor, and veracity, contradicted his evidence; and his chagrin can be imagined when the subaltern returned to duty, and received no punishment."(48) Probably adding to General Carr's unhappiness with the 11th Massachusetts was the fact that Lieutenant Colonel Porter D. Tripp, commanding officer of the 11th in Colonel William Blaisdell's absence, was the presiding officer of the court martial board.

The III Corps in Decline

When General Sickles lost his leg at Gettysburg, General William H. French was given the command of the III Corps. It was not a happy choice. After watching their new commander in action on a number of occasions, some of the men of the 11th Massachusetts were quite blunt in their opinions: "Here comes the old gin barrel!" "I should like to tap him." "His horse is drunk again today!"(49) A III Corps brigade commander, Colonel Regis DeTrobriand, wrote: "Near him a glass and a bottle of whiskey appeared to be on the table *en permanence,*" and concluded, "Poor III Corps! Your best days were over."(50) The more genteel spoke with irony of the III Corps "as we understand it."(51)

So far as leadership was concerned, the First Division of the III Corps was in much better shape than the Second Division. General Birney had been given command of the First Division after General Kearny was killed at Chantilly in 1862, which gave it the advantage of continuous competent leadership.

Francis Walker, the historian of the II Corps, described General Birney:

> He was eminently a sagacious man; and had an excellent understanding of military principles. In temper he was signally cool and composed. So far as the closest observation could discover, his mental processes were not a bit less steady and equable in the heat of action and under the severest fire than of "a summer's evening in his tent." Among the officers of the army, generally, he was reputed somewhat cold and strongly ambitious. If as a commander he was lacking in anything, it was in "creative pugnacity," the capacity for getting thoroughly angry when struck. This, more than anything else, was the element lacking in McClellan's composition; and a dash more of animal satisfaction in drawing blood would have improved the soldierly quality of Birney. Taken all in all, he was one of our most successful generals from civil life.(52)

The Second Division, on the other hand, had a succession of commanders after General Hooker—Daniel Sickles, Hiram Berry and Andrew Humphreys. The commander after Gettysburg was General Henry Prince.

The veterans of the 11th Massachusetts seemed to approve of their new division commander, primarily because he was not a part of the French-Carr clique. General French had, in fact, had Prince arrested in October 1863 because he had allowed his division to take off their shoes while fording a river.(53) The 11th Massachusetts was still very touchy on the subject of fording streams fully shod.

A third division had been added to the III Corps after the battle of Gettysburg. This division, previously commanded by General French, had little combat experience, having been used primarily as garrison troops at Harpers Ferry, Winchester and Martinsburg.

With French elevated to the corps command by seniority, command of the new division was given to General Carr. The loss of Carr, in the view of many of the veteran officers and enlisted men of the Hooker Brigade, was the only good thing that had happened to them in recent months. In the fall of 1863 General Carr had already gotten into the good graces of General French, and his new division garnered all the safe and cushy

National Archives/
Gen. David B. Birney commanded the 1st Division (Kearny's red patch) of the III Corps 1862-64 and the 3rd Division of the II Corps in 1864. He commanded the X Corps briefly before his death in October 1864.

assignments. The veterans of the 11th Massachusetts called the Third Division the "lambs."(54)

The fragile relationship among generals French, Carr and Prince was further strained during the Mine Run campaign. General Meade launched an ambitious offensive against Lee's army on Thanksgiving Day 1863; this effort turned out to be another Union turkey. The plan was to strike quickly down Orange Turnpike before the Confederates could consolidate their two corps in the vicinity of Mine Run, but when the Union III Corps, which was blocking the VI Corps, turned up a day late, the element of surprise was lost. Meade's choice of an unfamiliar and little used ford across the Rapidan and the absence of a good road map or guide resulted in the III Corps taking the wrong road on two successive days, which brought about a premature battle with the Confederates at Locust Grove and gave General Lee more time to bring up his troops. The grand Union assault was wisely called off by Meade, acting on the advice of General Gouverneur K. Warren on the very cold morning of November 30, and the Army of the Potomac was fortunate to fall back across the Rapidan without further misadventures.

Meade blamed General French, who blamed General Prince, who blamed General Carr and his division of lambs for the fiasco. Thus, there was finger pointing about Mine Run as well as the usual promotion politics and general back-biting at the III Corps winter camp at Brandy Station. And the infighting was exacerbated by General Meade's decision to reorganize the Union army.

II. In Camp at Brandy Station

The Battle of the Colonels of the 11ths

The trauma of reorganization added to an already tense situation of appointment politics at Brandy Station during the winter of 1863-1864. An intense struggle developed within the Hooker Brigade as to who would command it. When General Carr got his new division, he left "his brigade" to Colonel Robert McAllister, his close friend who was then the regimental commander of the 11th New Jersey.(55) Their plan went astray when Colonel William Blaisdell, who had commanded the 11th Massachusetts since just after First Bull Run, returned from sick leave and claimed command of the brigade by right of seniority. Blaisdell prevailed just before the Mine Run campaign, and a disgruntled McAllister returned to his regiment. He later asserted that in the subsequent months at Brandy Station, Blaisdell had "tyrannized" both him and General Carr.

There are two strikingly different views of what happened at Brandy Station in the winter and spring of 1864, and determining the good guys from the bad guys, if indeed that is possible, is left to the reader.

Robert McAllister of the 11th New Jersey and William Blaisdell of the 11th Massachusetts were very different in style, temperament and habits. Their infighting was intense. McAllister considered Blaisdell unfit and lacking in all moral values: "I don't know how a man of his caliber in tactics and morals could get such a position." He wrote further that

I think him totally unfit for the position, though I am not at liberty to say so. I have been recommended for a Brevet for gallantry by Gen. Carr and Gen. Humphreys; but that is the last I have heard of it. This is poor encouragement for an officer who has everything in the way of danger.

Library of Congress
Maj. Gen. William H. French, III Corps Commander (1863-64), was known to the troops as "Old Gin Barrel" or "Winky Blinky."

National Archives
Gen. Henry Prince, Commander of the Second Division (Hooker-White Diamond), III Corps (1863-64).

Blaisdell was not at Gettysburg. He was absent five months on some frivolous pretense. His appointment may not prevent mine; but it lessens my chance, as but a few will be appointed to fill existing vacancies which, I believe, is not numerous. Well, I shall discharge my duty to my country. I would rather be right than do wrong to get promoted.(56)

Colonel Blaisdell, let it be noted, had a chronic bronchial condition throughout the war which flared up in June of 1863. He was on sick leave at a hospital in Alexandria at the time of Gettysburg.

One of the fundamental differences between the two was the use of alcohol. Thomas D. Marbaker, the historian of the 11th New Jersey, wrote that McAllister

was known as a sincere Christian, but of rather a puritanical bent, and strongly opposed the use of intoxicants in any form. It was rarely, and on only extraordinary occasions, that he would allow it to be issued to the men. . . . Blaisdell, on the other hand, was not particularly known as

MOLLUS-USAMHI
Col. Robert McAllister, commander of the 11th New Jersey, was nicknamed "Mother McAllister."

National Archives
Col. William Blaisdell, commander of the 11th Massachusetts, was nicknamed "Old Cruelty."

a teetotaler, and did not object to the men having their regular ration of stimulants. Though both colonels were brave and gallant, they could not, because of disparity of tastes and dispositions, become very warm friends.(57)

Regis DeTrobriand, a fellow brigade commander in the Third Division later in 1864, gave this favorable appraisal of McAllister:

[He] is a character truly original. From what I have related of his services in front of the enemy, the reader would doubtless be led to imagine him as hard fighters are generally represented—still young, with loud voice, fierce mustache, lofty step, etc. Nothing could be further from the truth. McAllister is a good *pater familias,* having passed his [fiftieth] year. His voice is soft and calm; never, never on any occasion is it raised to the pitch of an oath or anything resembling it. Not only is his mustache not twisted, but his face is as closely shaven as that of an honest pastor. Everything about him has the air of simplicity and modesty. His habits are those of an anchorite. A temperance man, he never touches liquor of any kind, not even beer. Tolerant as to others, rigid for himself, he preaches by example only. His staff had full liberty to use moderately the liquors he refused himself, and it seemed perfectly a matter of course to him, when we visited him, that his adjutant, Major Frinkelmeyer, should offer us "the stirrup cup."

As punctual in his religious habits as he was severe in his belief, he had Protestant religious services regularly on Sunday at his headquarters. The most pleasant attention we could pay him was, on that day, to listen to the sermon of his chaplain.

His habitual kind-heartedness for the soldier did not affect his discipline. When he personally intervened in a punishment, he seldom failed to accompany it with a reprimand, the tenor and tone of which recalled to the culprit the scoldings he had received from his mother in his childhood. So that the soldiers among themselves called him affectionately "Mother McAllister." But when the day of battle came the mother led on her children as a lioness her cubs. Because he was a most exemplary man, McAllister was none the less the most energetic soldier.(58)

In his introduction to McAllister's letters, the editor writes of "those brigadiers and colonels whose quiet efficiency and resolute gallantry ultimately proved the salvation of the Union" and states that Colonel McAllister belonged "to that noble class."(59) It can be argued that Blaisdell was also a member of this noble class, but to lump these two men together would be upsetting to both.

When he was eighteen, Blaisdell enlisted in the 4th Infantry Regiment of the regular army and served for sixteen years. He fought in the Indian and Mexican wars, rose to sergeant, and served on General Winfield Scott's staff. He was wounded charging a battery in the Mexican War. On his discharge he was appointed an inspector in the Boston customs house. At the advent of the Civil War he was offered a commission as a captain in the regular army by General Scott but decided to enter the volunteer service.(60)

Very little published material exists on Blaisdell, but an unpublished portion of Henry Blake's memoirs expands our knowledge of his life. Blake points out that Blaisdell had been recommended for brigadier general by generals Hooker, Sickles and Winfield Scott Hancock, but Senator Charles Sumner and Governor John A. Andrew of Massachusetts were "hostile because he was coarse and profane in language, ignorant and discourteous."(61) Blake did not dissent from the appraisal but objected strongly that this was used as a basis for denying the promotion. He wrote that

some of the best fighting officers I was under were ignorant and degraded, unworthy associates in peace, but heroic, obedient and faithful in the performance of duty at the cannon's mouth.(62)

Henry Blake was as strongly against the use of alcohol as was McAllister, holding that

the total prohibition of the use of intoxicating liquor for any purpose or class of persons in the army would have preserved the lives of thousands, and shortened the duration of this war at least one year. The careful reader has noticed that the shameful drunkenness of a corps commander [French] became the stumbling block to victory, when Gen. Meade was foiled in the movement which terminated at Mine Run.(63)

Blake further wrote that at Spotsylvania, just before he was wounded, he counted

twenty-six general and staff officers that rode upon their horses with great difficulty on account of intoxication; my minutes contain notices of drunkenness upon every scene of conflict in which I was engaged. To avert unjust suspicion, I desire to state, that none of the officers with the regiment [11th Massachusetts] were rendered inefficient by this cause, in such important crises.(64)

The definition of "important crises" should be viewed taking into account the following Blaisdell story from Blake's unpublished memoirs:

A military demonstration [at Morton's Ford] was made by the II and III Corps in February, 1864, and the Colonel of the Regiment was assigned to the command of the Brigade and I acted as his Assistant Adjutant General. The orders designated the route and places to be occupied and plats of the country were prepared by the engineers for the guidance of the commanders of the march. A driving snow storm chilled the troops, and the Colonel was obfuscated by an overdose of fire water in his efforts to keep warm, but he could sit on his horse moving at a slow walk. A halt was ordered twelve miles from winter quarters near a small church near a fork of the roads, and the Brigade Commander looked silently several minutes at his plat, and then swore about the ignorant fool who didn't know what he was doing when marking the route. I noticed at a glance with my eagle eye that the paper was held upside down, and when it was handed to me corrected the error by holding it rightside up, and showing the highway to a ford on the Rapidan. We bivouacked while the snow was falling fast . . . [and] the serenity of the night was not broken by the rude tocsin of war. When I awoke in the morning, the Colonel was sitting by the camp fire and studying the plat which persisted in staying wrong side up. His mental condition was unchanged, and he asked, "Blake, how in hell did you hold this damn thing last night?" I replied promptly by rotating the papers with my fingers. "Blake," he exclaimed, "I always want you on my staff. You are always sober when the rest of us are drunk." After returning to the camp at Brandy Station, Virginia, the Colonel and I prepared the official report of the movements of the Brigade, which is in my handwriting and filed in the archives of the War Department. I confess most humbly the whole truth does not appear therein, but I remember I was thanked profusely for my valuable services as Assistant Adjutant General.(65)

After commenting on Blaisdell's liberal use of drink and profanity, Blake reported an essential point and somewhat balanced the scale:

This is an appropriate place to refer to another phase of Colonel Blaisdell and mention his soldierly qualities, his conspicuous bravery, and practical and essential knowledge of actual warfare. The test of a soldier is not merely popularity, but the ability to keep cool and direct under fire, and face without flinching the foe and inspire his followers by example.(66)

The McAllister letters suggest that the lax discipline when Blaisdell was in command contributed significantly to his failure to receive a brigadier's promotion. There seems to be little evidence to support such a conclusion. Blake wrote that General Hancock told him after the war that Colonel Blaisdell was known as "Old Cruelty" because he was such a strict disciplinarian. Recommendations for his promotion were made throughout his military career, including one on the eve of the reorganization and courts martial.(67)

Life at Brandy Station—Not Without Amusement

Camp life at Brandy Station included some rather elaborate social events. McAllister noted that Colonel Blaisdell "is the party that was prominent and conspicuous in taking the church for a dance hall."(68) Sergeant Marbaker of the 11th New Jersey was less critical of the dance hall operation than his colonel. He noted that the officers were able to bring their wives and daughters to the "grand balls" at Brandy Station during the winter, but this option was not open to the enlisted men. They were forced to improvise. He reported that

> a dance without something resembling femininity not being very attractive, the want was filled by dressing in female garb the youngest and most effeminate soldiers. Some sent North for female apparel, but as that was not always practicable, many ways were resorted to and many varieties of material used to get up costumes. Colonel McAllister, no doubt, would have been very indignant had he known that one of his table-covers sometimes figured as a skirt upon George W. Lindley, the writer's "steady company." . . . The season closed with a grand conflagration. Some incendiary fired the building, and in spite of the heroic efforts of the New York firemen, from the Excelsior Brigade, who quickly had their machines on the spot—said machines consisting of the running-gears of baggage-wagons with ropes attached—the building was entirely consumed. No insurance.(69)

The ability of the officers "to live it up" to a degree at Brandy Station was not dwelt upon by McAllister in his letters. His good friend General Carr, with his dancing master background, was a social leader which may have impressed Chief of Staff Andrew Humphreys, if not General Meade. Lieutenant Colonel Theodore Lyman of Meade's staff gave the following account of General Humphreys' social activities when one winter day Humphreys wanted Lyman to help him in entertaining a group of thirteen ladies who had arrived at Brandy Station on the train. Lyman wrote that he

> put on the double-breaster, added a cravat, and proceeded, with a sweet smile, to the tent, whence came a sound of revelry and champagne corks. Such a set of feminine humans I have not seen often; it was Lowell factories broken loose and gone mad. They were all gotten up in some sort of long thing, to ride in. One had got a lot of orange tape and trimmed

Historical Society of Pennsylvania

General Humphreys' Happy Hour.

her jacket in the dragoon style; another had the badge of the III Corps pinned all askew in her hat; a third had a major's knot worked in tarnished lace on her sleeve; while a fourth had garnitured her chest by a cape of grey squirrel-skin. And there was General Humphreys, very red in the face, smiling like a basket of chips, and hopping round with a champagne bottle, with all the spring of a boy of sixteen.(70)

Lyman was then asked to go with General Humphreys and the ladies to General John Sedgwick's headquarters of the VI Corps.

But Uncle John, though blushing and overcome, evidently did not choose to be put upon; so, with great politeness, he offered them sherry, with naught to eat and champagne. Then nothing would do but go to Headquarters of the III Corps [French], whither, to my horror, the gallant Humphreys would gang likewise.

. . . Finally one lady's horse ran away, and off went the brick, Humphreys, like a shot, to stop her. Seeing her going into a pine tree, he drove his horse between the tree and her; but, in so doing, encountered a hidden branch, which slapped the brisk old gent out of his saddle, like

Original drawing by Tim Buckett
The Ladies Have Arrived—General Carr's III Corps Ball.

a shuttle-cock! The Chief-of-Staff was up in a second, laughing at his mishap; while I galloped up, in serious alarm at his accident. To make short a long story, the persistent H. tagged after those womenfolk (and I tagged after him) first to Corps Headquarters, then to General Carr's Headquarters, and finally to General [William Hopkins] Morris's Headquarters [one of Carr's Brigade commanders], by which time it was dark! I was the only one that knew the nearest way home (we were four miles away) and didn't I lead the eminent soldier through runs and mud-holes, the which he do hate!(71)

General Carr threw the first ball of the social season at Brandy Station in the winter of 1864. Humphreys described the affair:

What a ride we had over to General Carr's headquarters where a ball took place. What a flounder rather, I should say, through the mud. But we did get there and found an immense ball room, well filled. It was a temporary structure of canvas, the side covered with flags. Three bands were at one end. There was no attempt at dressing on the part of ladies who went in for the enjoyment of dancing. Midlength of the hall at a

A General on the Move—Drawings by C.W. Newton, New York, 1863

Gen. Carr's head-quarters at Licking Run, November 4, 1863. *(National Archives)*

Gen. Carr's head-quarters at Brandy Station, November 16, 1863. *(National Archives)*

Gen. Carr's head-quarters at Brandy Station, December 8, 1863. *(National Archives)*

Library of Congress

General Carr's last headquarters at Brandy Station (Dec. 8, 1863 to the reorganization) and the site of the ball, was the mansion called "Sunbright," a part of the Daniel Kennedy farm. It was destroyed in 1988 by a developer.

Library of Congress

Typical Union officer's hut, Army of the Potomac, at Brandy Station, winter 1864-65.

proper time a curtain rolled up and showed a long line of profusely covered tables. The supper was of the most abundant kind; plenty of wines. I enjoyed the affair to a certain degree.

There were some interesting ladies, fragile looking creatures who at three o'clock in the morning wished the ball would continue until ten. It was after four o'clock when we got home.(72)

The New York *Herald*'s correspondent wrote:

The first army ball of the season is to come off near the headquarters of General Carr. . . . The house [Sunbright] is large and commodious, and stands directly beside the railway, about one mile south of Brandy Station, and in sight on the residence of John M. Botts. A ball-room, eighty feet by sixty, is being added, and supper has been ordered for a large number of guests. The President, Secretary of War, and General [Henry Wager] Halleck are among the invited guests. A special train will be run to carry the ladies directly to the house, where platforms and walks have been laid to protect them from the mud.(73)

Lincoln, Stanton and Halleck did not attend, but Generals French, Birney and Humphreys did. Interestingly, General Prince is not noted as being in attendance. Carr's ball was held on January 26th at a cost estimated to be $2,000. Not to be outdone, the officers of the II Corps followed with an even more festive affair, in a larger ballroom, on Washington's Birthday.(74)

Religion at Brandy Station

Colonel McAllister, his letters indicate, spent a great deal of his time attending Christian meetings, supporting the work of the Christian Commission, evaluating chaplains, and generally trying to improve the spiritual well-being of his regiment. He did not approve of the moral tone of the 11th Massachusetts and that of the Hooker Brigade after Colonel Blaisdell replaced him as its commander.

The view of the 11th Massachusetts, as expressed by Henry Blake, was one of some skepticism about the efficacy of these religious efforts. In his book Blake frequently referred to a chaplain prosecuted for stealing a horse, wrote

National Archives

Headquarters of the Christian Commission, Germantown. During 1864, the commission's "faithful, zealous and indefatigable delegates" distributed 47,103 boxes of hospital stores and 569,594 Bibles and testaments. They also erected 205 chapels and chapel tents.

at some length on the uselessness of Christian Commission religious tracts, and noted that the Christian Commission pulled the roof from the chapel that had been built by the enlisted men.

> An agent of the Christian Commission furnished a capacious tent which formed the roof; and religious, temperance and Masonic meetings were frequently held, until this apostle, who employed most of his time in writing long letters for the press, that portrayed in vivid colors the "good work" which he was accomplishing, removed the canvas because the innocent social assembly occupied it during one evening.(75)

It does appear that the Massachusetts regiment was a rowdier group than the 11th New Jersey. This may have been due, to some degree, to the caliber of their spiritual advisers. Blake reported that the bishop of Massachusetts had apologized to him for their chaplain. His recommendation had been based on the word of another bishop, but having received complaints about the man, an investigation "ascertained his main business was raising chickens and he was noted for his extreme acquisitiveness in many matters."(76) Blake recorded his opinion of Elisha F. Watson, chaplain of the 11th Massachusetts:

I did not hear more than five sermons during my term of service, and the Chaplains with rare exceptions like Messrs. Cudworth [of the 1st Massachusetts] and Humphrey [unidentified], did not earn the respect of the men. The love of the root of evil was the ruling passion of our Chaplain, who provided and cooked meals for the field and staff officers of the 11th, and Col. Blaisdell threatened several times to punish him when dinner was not satisfactory by ordering him to preach on the following Sunday. The Chaplain had one redeeming quality, courage in a high degree, and should have been a Captain of Infantry. I listened to an argument by the officers on some topic and the Chaplain easily vanquished Lieut. Col. Tripp, who was mad and roared, "I don't want any words with you, you damned old hypocrite." This mild language was in comparison with the vile profanity which daily greeted the ears of visitors at regimental headquarters. The Chaplain of a New York regiment was present on a certain afternoon, staggering under his load of whiskey and reported Col. Blaisdell for swearing. The Col. answered with an oath, "It's no worse for me to swear than for you to get drunk." And the Chaplain boasted without blushing, "I was brought up on a bottle and never saw any harm in it." The soldiers were demoralized by exhibitions of this unseemly character and ceased to show proper reverence.(77)

Blake described Watson's brief career and dismissal.

The Chaplain preached one sermon on Faith and another on Hope, and then reported his valise and fifty sermons were stolen and the contents were never recovered. He said they were products of twenty years of study and labor and did not preach again to the 11th. I am satisfied the thieves were commissioned officers on a spree, but the rank and file and fair minded soldiers denounced the conduct as low and despicable. Our Chaplain was finally and justly dismissed for the good of the service by order of President Lincoln.(78)

Meade's Reorganization of the Army

On March 25, 1864, during their train trip from Boston to the camp at Brandy Station, Private Samuel Blood and his fellow travelers, new recruits in the Union army, were transferred to a brigade, division and corps different from the ones they were originally assigned to. This probably meant very little to Blood and his compatriots, but to the veterans of the Hooker Brigade it meant a great deal.

Meade's reorganization of the Army of the Potomac eliminated the I and III Corps. The old Hooker and Kearny Divisions of the III Corps were assigned to the II Corps, commanded by General Winfield Scott Hancock. The Hooker Brigade was abolished, and the 11th Massachusetts was assigned to the Excelsior Brigade, previously comprising New York regiments, which was commanded by Colonel William Brewster. Colonel Blaisdell reverted to regimental command of the 11th Massachusetts. The reorganization was accompanied by the appointment of Joseph B. Carr as the new Hooker Division commander, a decision repugnant to the old regiments of the Hooker Brigade, the 11th Massachusetts in particular.(79)

[Ed. note: For a complete chart of the reorganized units, see Appendix A.]

Although they did not hold protest meetings, the Kearny-Birney Division was also irate. They erected a wooden "head stone" constructed by one of its regiments in a mock cemetery.(80)

General Carr's lambs, now under General James Ricketts, were assigned to the VI Corps. Blake wrote that their "subsequent service under brave leaders" rectified its tarnished history under a "drunkard" corps commander

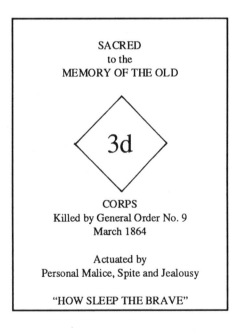

SACRED
to the
MEMORY OF THE OLD

3d

CORPS
Killed by General Order No. 9
March 1864

Actuated by
Personal Malice, Spite and Jealousy

"HOW SLEEP THE BRAVE"

Under the Red Patch: Story of the 63rd Pa. Volunteers, by Gilbert A. Hays

Wooden "headstone" erected to memorialize the passing of the III Corps.

41

USAMHI

Major General George G. Meade and staff, the reorganizers, in September 1863, at Culpeper, Virginia, near Brandy Station. Gen. Andrew A. Humphreys, Chief of Staff, (hatless) faces Gen. Meade. Lt. Col. Theodore Lyman is at far right.

and the "cowardice" of its previous division commander. The existence of the "drunkard" corps commander, General French, may have played a crucial role in the demise of the III Corps.

In memoirs written after the war, Blake noted his closeness to Senator Henry Wilson of Massachusetts, who later was Grant's first term vice president:

> I made the acquaintance of the "Natick Cobbler" in the fifties and met him during the war and afterwards, and cheerfully present some qualities of that high minded statesman which merit praise. He was ready to engage in conversation and alert in putting questions relating to the army and learning the opinion of any soldier, high or low in rank, and it was understood this was his method of acquiring information as a politician, or as Chairman of the Senate Committee on Military Affairs. The Senator welcomed everybody, kept his eyes and ears open and honored all with respectful attention. I was a Sergeant eleven months and while in this humble rank, he discussed with me grave problems confronting the nation as if I were his colleague.

... The confidential nature of my intercourse with Sen. Wilson, (and I was not alone), can be shown by one instance when the disaster at Mine Run and behavior of Gen. Wm. H. French were under consideration. . . I admitted the truth of the disgraceful charges against its commander and our interview concluded with this prediction: "Gen. French has a host of powerful friends and cannot be removed from his command, and the III Corps will be broken up and the Divisions assigned to other Corps before the next campaign."(81)

The reorganization's elimination of both the I and III Corps was based on a number of rationales independent of French's removal. Meade believed that neither corps had really recovered from Gettysburg, and because there were so many corps in the Army of the Potomac it had reduced the ability of the commander to adequately control his troops. The idea was that bigger is better. Unfortunately, his theory would be tested in the Wilderness, where control of even the smallest units would be a problem.

General Meade's Chief of Staff, General Humphreys, wrote some time after the war:

[T]he three infantry corps [in the Army of the Potomac] amounted to 73,390 officers and enlisted men, giving an average strength of nearly 25,000 to each. In a country so heavily wooded as that in which the operations were to be conducted, five infantry corps of about 15,000 each would have been a more judicious organization, owing to the difficulty of communication between the corps commanders in a battle in such a country, and the consequent difficulty of prompt and efficient control of lines of battle.(82)

General Alexander S. Webb, commander of one of the "heavy" brigades in General John Gibbon's Division of the II Corps, who was in the thick of the fighting in the Wilderness, also wrote later:

Besides causing great dissatisfaction throughout the army, the consolidation in my opinion, was the indirect cause of much of the confusion in the execution of orders, and the handling of troops during the battles of the Wilderness.(83)

Actually, in the second day of fighting in the Wilderness, the II Corps troops were split into two commands under Generals Birney and Gibbon, along with a hodge-podge of units from the V, VI and IX Corps, all under the overall command of Hancock. It made a confusing organization chart.

The fact that the reorganization on March 25 came so close to the spring offensive exacerbated the situation. The regiment, brigades and divisions in the main stayed in their original camps—probably a wise decision considering the lateness of the hour—but this could hardly have increased command coordination and cohesiveness.

At the end of March, all that the Hooker Brigade veterans knew was that there was no III Corps and no Hooker Brigade, but there was Joseph Bradford Carr as their division commander. In hollow consolation, they were allowed to keep the distinctive diamond patch of their beloved division and brigade. In a parade before General Grant, one unit proudly displayed their old insignia on their hats and relegated their new II Corps badge to the seat of their pants.(84)

III. The Mutiny and Courts Martial

The Meeting

With some of the officers of the 11th Massachusetts as the primary organizers, a protest meeting to vent their injured feelings was arranged on March 25. The participants were some thirty to fifty junior officers, no one above captain, from five of the regiments of the Hooker Brigade: the 11th and 16th Massachusetts, the 11th New Jersey, and the 26th and 84th Pennsylvania. Colonel McAllister wrote that no officers of the 11th New Jersey participated, other than to oppose the meeting,(85) but the courts martial transcripts show otherwise.

There is no evidence that any officers of the 1st Massachusetts, a charter member of the Hooker Brigade, took part and no mention is made of the affair in Chaplain Cudworth's history of that regiment.(86) Politics and clique formation may be the answer. Another may be that the commanding officer of the 1st Massachusetts, Colonel Napoleon Bonaparte McLaughlen, had been

Library of Congress
Col. N.B. McLaughlen, Commander of the 1st Massachusetts, may have spared his officers from arrest because of his earlier encounter with Gen. Prince.

Original drawing by Tim Buckett

Five participants of the protest meeting were arrested and transported to headquarters in a freight wagon while Gen. Carr looked on approvingly.

brought before a court martial board by General Prince a few months previously. The charge had a slightly bureaucratic ring: returning to duty some deserters without proper notice or authorization of the commanding general. The court martial board, with General Carr presiding, acquitted the colonel and criticized General Prince for bringing the charges.(87) In the Byzantine goings-on at Brandy Station, McLaughlen's officers perhaps were happier with the Carr appointment than those of some of the other regiments.

The Arrests and Charges

A couple of days after the meeting, five of the participants were placed under arrest. Four officers of the 11th Massachusetts—lieutenants Henry Blake and George Forrest, and captains James R. Bigelow and Walter Smith—and Captain E. C. Thomas of the 26th Pennsylvania were loaded into a wagon, French Revolution style. They were transported under the guard of ten enlisted men to II Corps headquarters for trials for mutiny and violations of military discipline. Colonel McAllister, overjoyed with these developments, wrote:

Library of Congress
Gen. Winfield Scott Hancock, II Corps Commander 1863-64, ordered the court martial board to convene.

MOLLUS-USAMHI
Lt. Col. Francis Walker, Asst. Adj. Gen. of the II Corps, brought the charges. He later became the II Corps historian.

[S]o far as it regards the breaking up of the Brigade, and the placing of my regiment in the old Jersey Brigade, I am not only satisfied; but pleased. General [Gershom] Mott is a good brigade commander and a gentleman and it relieves me from that poor miserable creature, Col. Blaisdell. He has to return to his regiment and is hopping mad. I am rejoiced and so are all my friends. I have laughed more than I have for a month at this turn of events, breaking up that abominable clique and returning them to their regiments and companies. It is said that Col. Blaisdell and his friends are all under arrest. I am glad of it. My friend, Genl. Carr, commands our Division. I am right among my friends and am happy.(88)

In a later letter McAllister stated that he was saddened by the fact that Colonel Blaisdell was not also arrested. "They have only caught his tools."(89)

The charges against the officers had been filed by General Carr, but they were brought by the headquarters of the II Corps. The special order appointing

MOLLUS-USAMHI
Gen. Gershom Mott commanded the
3rd Brigade, 2d Division, III Corps 1863-
64. After the reorganization, he commanded the ill-fated 4th Division in the
Wilderness and at Spotsylvania.

John W. Kuhl Collection
Lt. Col. John Schoonover succeeded
Col. McAllister as commander of the
11th New Jersey.

the convening of the court martial board was by order of General Winfield Scott
Hancock, commander of the II Corps, and signed by Lieutenant Colonel Francis
A. Walker, the assistant adjutant general. Hancock had just returned to the II
Corps from a second recuperation period necessitated by his Gettysburg wound,
and the details of the reorganization were new to him, particularly the politics
and persona of his new III Corps divisions. Ironically, Francis Walker is the
same commentator who wrote long after the war:

> Of the grief and anger of the officers and men of the III Corps at the
> dismemberment of that noble body of troops, with which they had been
> so long connected, of which they had justly been so proud, and which
> had become to them a sacred thing, it is not meet to speak here. That
> wound has never yet wholly healed in the heart of many a brave and
> patriotic soldier. Certain it is that, since the break must come, these old
> divisions of Kearny and Hooker could not have been sent to any body

of troops where their gallantry and discipline would have been more cordially recognized, or where they would have found heartier comradeship.(90)

The charges were drawn up by Captain Henry Harrison Bingham of Hancock's staff, a twenty-two-year-old lawyer who had just graduated from Washington and Jefferson College when he joined the army in August 1862. The transcripts of the court martial reveal how the charges originated. After the protest meeting, a group of officers of the 11th New Jersey met in Colonel McAllister's tent with the acting commander of the regiment, Lieutenant Colonel John Schoonover, and it was decided to report to General Carr on what had transpired at the meeting. Then Carr and Bingham put together the charges, with the 11th New Jersey officers who attended the meeting as the prosecution witnesses. McAllister was on leave in New Jersey when this transpired. He returned to camp a couple of days before the trials opened.

The most serious charges were against Captain Bigelow. The first was that he "did incite a Mutiny by publicly advocating" in a meeting "by speech and vote for a motion that a Committee be appointed to draft resolutions to express the disgust of the Division with regard to the contemplated alterations in the Corps" and that he assisted in organizing the meeting "thereby tending to create discontent among the soldiers and disquiet and dissatisfaction in the Army." The second charge was that he had shown contemptuous and disrespectful conduct to this superior officer, Brigadier General Carr, in that he spoke of him in the following language:

It was a God-damned outrage to break up this Division for the purpose of relieving Col. Blaisdell of his command, and Genl. Carr is at the bottom of it; Genl. Carr is a "damned cowardly son of a bitch and damned rascal," or words to that effect.

The rest of the officers were charged with insubordinate conduct to the prejudice of good order and military discipline.

The Protest Resolution

One problem for the prosecution was that the charges were somewhat at odds with the contents of the resolution that was adopted at the meeting. The resolution dealt wholly with the brigade and appears quite innocuous, except for the provision for its transmission to the press and the Congress, something that will always get the attention of the higher military echelons. It appears that neither the notice and minutes of the meeting, nor the resolution adopted, had been obtained prior to the trial. The resolution, in Henry Blake's own hand, stated in part:

> Whereas, the First Brigade, Second Division, III Corps, has been so reorganized as to destroy its original identity, therefore
>
> Resolved: That it is with deep regret we have heard that the Government have considered it necessary to dissolve us and sunder the ties which have bound us together as a military organization since the commencement of the war, and whose record, we hope, does us no dishonor.
>
> Resolved: That, while we are willing to submit to any order which the General Commanding the Army deems it expedient to promulgate, we respectfully request, if not incompatible with the interests of the service, that this Brigade, (if not the oldest, one of the oldest in the Volunteer service), may be retained as an organization for the few remaining months of its period of service.
>
> Resolved: That, as the Government has dissolved this old Brigade, we, as officers, will in good faith serve our distressed country to the best of our ability during the balance of our term of service, and will do our best wherever we may be placed, and under whoever we may be ordered to serve, so long as he be a lover of American Liberties and the Constitution of the United States.

The Court

The blue ribbon court martial board included officers of great reputation in the Army of the Potomac:

MOLLUS-USAMHI
Library of Congress

Capt. Henry H. Bingham, judge advocate on Gen. Hancock's staff, conducted the prosecution.

Gen. Alexander Hays, commander of
the 2nd Brigade, 3rd Division, II Corps.,
was the initial presiding officer.

> Brigadier General Alexander Hays, U.S. Volunteers, commanding
> officer, Second Brigade, Third Division, the presiding officer
> Colonel William R. Brewster, commanding officer, Excelsior
> (Second) Brigade, Fourth Division
> Lieutenant Colonel Waldo Merriam, commanding officer, 16th
> Massachusetts
> Major Peter Nelson, 66th New York
> Major Henry L. Abbott, commanding officer, 20th Massachusetts
> Captain Isaac W. Starbird, 19th Maine
> Captain William McAllister, 140th Pennsylvania
> Captain James Hamilton, 105th Pennsylvania

General Hays had also been adversely affected by the reorganization, and
initially was quite bitter about losing his division command. His Third Division
of the II Corps was eliminated, and its regiments were folded into other II Corps
divisions. Hays wrote to his wife on March 25:

> An attempt is being made to reorganize, and so far it has been worse than
> a farce.... The III Corps has been broken up, but to complete the sacrifice

MOLLUS-USAMHI

Col. W. R. Brewster, commander of the Excelsior Brigade, presided at the last four courts martial.

Massachusetts Historical Society

Lt. Col. Waldo Merriam, commander of the 16th Massachusetts, was challenged as a judge by the defense for alleged bias.

the Third Division, II Corps, is called upon to disband. The noble old organization still survives, and I am still its commander, but in a few days I fear it will be like "the baseless fabric of a vision."

The enemies of our country have, in time past, assailed it in vain, and now it dissolves by the action of our own friends. Apropos, "Save me from friends, and I will take care of my enemies."(91)

A second irony is that at this very time General Hays was contesting the appointment of General Carr. He based his claim to division command on his earlier appointment by the President and the fact that "I am fully as well identified with that corps (the III) under General [Samuel P.] Heintzelman and the lamented Kearny as any officer in it."(92)

On April 1, "All Fool's Day in honor of my patron saint," General Hays wrote to his wife,

I am busy, "head over ears." Today I rode to corps headquarters and assembled the court-martial, of which I am president, and returned this

MOLLUS-USAMHI
Maj. Henry L. Abbott, commander of the
20th Massachuestts, served as a judge
for the courts martial.

Roger Hunt Collection
Capt. Isaac Starbird, 19th Maine,
served as a judge for the courts martial.

evening, tired and hungry, although Hancock pressed his hospitality
upon me. The court was "large and respectable," like ancient Democratic
meetings, evidently selected for grit and fearlessness in discharge of
duty.

I was, however, surprised when I learned that we had convened for
the trial of five commissioned officers, charged with mutiny, a consequence of the reorganization of the army. The extreme penalty of this
offense, if proven, is death.(93)

The Trial of Captain James R. Bigelow

The first officer to be tried was Captain James R. Bigelow who the prosecution thought was the ring leader behind the meeting. Bigelow, a bookseller
in Boston before the war, had raised Company E of the 11th Massachusetts
from a militia unit, the Boston Light Guard, on April 16, 1861.(94)

53

Original Drawing by Tim Buckett

Capt. Bigelow's court martial. From left, Capt. Starbird, Maj. Abbott, Col. Brewster and Gen. Hays (judges); Col. Blaisdell (witness); Judge Advocate Bingham (seated); defense attorney Blake; defendant Bigelow (seated); and judges Maj. Nelson, Capt. Hamilton and Capt. McAllister (partly hidden from view).

McAllister, as would be expected, held a very negative view of the captain:

When I commanded the old Brigade, I got Captain Bigelow his position as Inspector General. After Blaisdell came into power, Bigelow was ready and willing to do his dirty work. He has thus been caught in his own trap. A common saying here is that Capt. Bigelow has as many faces as a State House clock, which I know to be very true.(95)

Colonel Blaisdell, testifying as a defense witness, said he had known Bigelow for seventeen years and that he had never been arrested in the army. Asked about his performance at Chancellorsville, Blaisdell stated,

He was Acting Major; he performed his duty first rate. I saw him rallying the men and he was severely wounded while in the line of duty in that battle.(96)

Defendant Bigelow's first move was to petition the court to appoint Lieutenant Blake as defense counsel. Captain Bingham objected but was overruled with the proviso that Blake could not also be called as a witness.

The courts martial transcripts reflect none of the interplay between members of the court and counsels, other than when arguing a legal point. Blake wrote in his unpublished memoirs:

MOLLUS-USAMHI
Capt. James R. Bigelow, 11th Massachusetts, was the first defendant to face the panel of judges.

I expected the Court Martial would be a dignified and formal body, but the members relaxed and the proceedings were interrupted by irrelevant comments.... Most of the members were warm partisans of Gen. [George] McClellan, and on one morning an article was read in a newspaper, stating that some parties had presented a sword to Gen. Grant, and Maj. Abbott, whom I knew in Harvard, said, "Gen. Grant has not done anything to deserve a sword, Gen. McClellan [everything?]." This appeared to be the sentiment of the majority and I gave my view boldly and perhaps disrespectfully. "If I uttered language like that, I should expect to be Court Martialled."(97)

It is doubtful that Hays felt that way about Grant, but Abbott was an avowed and vocal Democrat. His father, Josiah Abbott, was campaigning in Massachusetts against the incumbent abolitionist, Senator Sumner. Abbott in his letters often endorsed his father's views. For example, he wrote to his father in September of 1863:

I am so strongly impressed with the truth of every word you say about public matters that I can't help feeling devilish gloomy about the future.

There seems to be an awful feeling of indifference that will make it only too easy for somebody to usurp power in the course of events. Any army of aliens & conscripts can certainly be used to do any thing they are bidden. I don't see how there can be any reply to your argument about the (Emancipation) proclamation & your distinction between a government of men & of laws. But the trouble is (that) the large party of Abolitionists don't attempt to answer the arguments. They seem really indifferent to the danger & utterly unable to appreciate the results of the present system. Thank God, however, that in this regiment they are all unanimously on the right side. The few abolitionists in the army call this the copperhead regt.

Fortunately for the unanimity of the "right side," Blake had beaten Abbott into the service and was not in the 20th Massachusetts, known as the Harvard regiment because so many of its officers came from the college. In urging Oliver Wendell Holmes, Jr., not to return to the regiment before his latest wound had fully healed, Abbott wrote "If any impudent stay-at-home Wide-Awake asks you when you are coming back, punch his head."(98)

Wide-awake counsel Blake was surrounded by enemies but not intimidated. He immediately objected to Lieutenant Colonel Merriam serving on the court because he was biased against the defendant. Bigelow, as inspector general of the brigade, had questioned some of the actions of Merriams's regiment, the 16th Massachusetts. Although Merriam denied the allegation, he asked to be excused.

Blake also objected to the judge advocate in that he had not developed the case with the defendant's rights protected as required by the rules of courts martial. Each time an objection was made the court had to be cleared, the legal arguments made, and the decision rendered on the point at issue. Counsel Blake lost this one and most of his other objections and exceptions.(99)

All of the prosecution's witnesses were members of the 11th New Jersey. Second Lieutenant Alfred DuPaget of Company K was called first. Lieutenant DuPaget's military career presents a very mixed picture, from hero to alleged drunkard, malingerer, and perjurer. As a sergeant a year earlier, DuPaget had been cited for bravery by McAllister and given a commission as second lieutenant on the basis of his performance at Chancellorsville, but by the winter of 1863-1864 the situation was somewhat different. His military file shows that in March 1864 court martial charges were filed against him for "feigning sickness" to avoid picket duty and for "drunkenness" at a meeting of officers at the 11th Massachusetts' chapel. The witnesses included the three surgeons from the 11th Massachusetts, 11th New Jersey and the 16th Massachusetts,

Library of Congress
These surgeons of the Second Division, III Corps, are very likely the ones who certified Lt. Alfred DuPaget as a malingerer and sent him back to duty. From the left, unidentified; C.C. Jewitt, 16th Mass; E.C. Welling, 11th N.J.; and J.F. Calhoun, Division Surgeon.

whose findings were defended by Dr. J. F. Calhoun, the division medical director. Apparently these charges were never processed by the new management of the brigade and division. The record also shows that during this period DuPaget tried to resign his commission stating that his continued service was "aggravating" the condition of his sick wife. He was unsuccessful as it "was too near the commencement of a campaign."(100)

The judge advocate questioned DuPaget about the object of the meeting and who had stated what it was. Blake objected on the ground that the judge advocate had not exercised proper diligence in getting the written minutes and resolutions which were the best evidence of the meeting's purpose. It was apparent that the prosecution, if it relied on the resolutions alone, had a very weak case.

Blake even objected to the questions as to whether the old Second Division of the III corps was now the Fourth Division of the II Corps since there was no official notice of the Meade reorganization on the record. The judge advocate said the order was still confidential and thus privileged. The court overruled the

Prosecution Witnesses

New Jersey State Archives

Acting Lt. Benjamin Morehouse, Company F, 11th New Jersey.

John W. Kuhl Collection

Capt. Samuel T. Sleeper, Company I, 11th New Jersey.

John W. Kuhl Collection

Acting 1st Lieut. William S. Rockhill, Co. I, 11th New Jersey as he appeared at the trial in an officer's uniform.

John W. Kuhl Collection

W. S. Rockhill uniformed as a sergeant major, as the defense contended he should have testified.

objection, but a copy of the reorganization order was ultimately put into the record.

DuPaget eventually gave his testimony about the meeting, which followed quite closely the specifications in the charges. He testified that captains William C. Allen and James R. Bigelow of the 11th Massachusetts and J. H. Smith of the 11th New Jersey had all declined to chair the meeting. Captain Edward C. Thomas of the 26th Pennsylvania finally volunteered, a decision he would come to regret.

Captain Allen's refusal to be the chairman was reasonable considering his circumstances. Just a few days earlier he had been convicted of conduct unbecoming an officer and a gentleman and was sentenced to be dismissed from the service.(101)

DuPaget testified that Bigelow had given the following excuse for not being the presiding officer:

He said something to the effect that he was in a very peculiar position so far as the meeting was concerned, but was sent there for some other purpose.

Bigelow would later testify that he was sent there to keep order. Colonel Blaisdell, called as a defense witness, generally supported this testimony:

I cannot say that I gave it as a positive order, I directed him to go. I think I told him to go to the meeting. He might have construed it into an order. The Captain told me there was going to be a meeting of the Division in the Hall in rear of the Brigade. I asked him the object of the meeting and he said as far as he had heard it was to be a friendly meeting as the Brigade was going to be broken up and put in new hands. . . . I told him that he had better go over and see that no altercation took place. There might be some drunken men present who would get the party into trouble.

DuPaget testified that Lieutenant Forrest, the quartermaster, had suggested that a committee of three should be appointed to draft some resolutions to carry out the objects of the meeting, which were to express the disgust of the Second Division with the contemplated alterations of the corps. DuPaget said that Lieutenant Smith of the 11th New Jersey seconded the motion. He further testified that after he had spoken in opposition to the resolution, Forrest said "he was willing to sign all he said in large letters." Then DuPaget, after another overruled defense objection, testified that the principal part taken in the meeting was by officers of the 11th Massachusetts Volunteers.

Judge Advocate Bingham then questioned DuPaget on the charge of disrespectful conduct. DuPaget testified that before the meeting he heard Bigelow, in a conversation with Captain Samuel T. Sleeper of Company I, 11th New Jersey, speak about General Carr's complicity in breaking up the division and about his cowardice in battle. He also said that Bigelow had declared that Carr had "owed Captain Cook $400 for commissary stores and that he, Captain Cook, could not get any of it."(102)

Finally, DuPaget said that four or five officers including Bigelow had voted for the motion, and he was the only officer who had voted against it.

The next witness for the prosecution was Sergeant Benjamin F. Morehouse, acting First Lieutenant of Company F, 11th New Jersey. Blake immediately objected to the witness appearing in the "uniform and equipment of a commissioned officer," stating that "there is no such rank as acting lieutenant." The court overruled the objection, saying the court would determine its own "dignity." Blake, in his own trial, noted that General Hays, off the record, had reprimanded Morehouse about wearing an officer's uniform.

Blake made his usual objections about parol (oral) testimony on a question about the object of the meeting from Bigelow's conversation with Sleeper. Again the court overruled the objection and stated that any further such motions would also be overruled. The court declared that the judge advocate had used "sufficient diligence to obtain the original records of the meeting." In other details Morehouse's testimony followed closely the words spelled out in the charges.

On cross examination, the defense pursued a line of questioning that may have been designed to show that Morehouse was not at the meeting. He was asked whether a dance had been held prior to the meeting; he didn't know. Blake asked whether he heard about "any resolutions that were adopted at the meeting, and if so, state the substance." The judge advocate objected to the question on the grounds that this matter had not been gone into on direct examination and, thus, the defense could not explore it on cross examination. The objection was sustained. Blake then rephrased the question, asking, "Did you hear any remarks about breaking up the corps?" Morehouse said no. He also said he didn't see Bigelow vote for the resolution. Obviously this was not the answer the judge advocate wanted on the record, and he asked Morehouse a question on redirect. "When you said you did not hear any remarks at the meeting about breaking up the Division you didn't mean to include Captain Bigelow's conversation with Captain Sleeper did you?" "No," was the answer to the leading question.

Probably the most damaging witness against Bigelow was Samuel Sleeper. In a letter to his wife, McAllister noted that he had spent the preceding evening with Sleeper at a prayer meeting and that the captain "makes a most excellent prayer."(103) When Sleeper was called as a witness, Blake noted that Hays said immediately "one of a family of seven."(104) This irrelevant comment is subject to a number of interpretations.

Captain Sleeper testified that Captain Bigelow told him,

"Ain't this a damned outrage the breaking up the old Division." He said, "Joe Carr is at the bottom of the whole of it." I am not so positive of this part of it, but I think he said it was to get Blaisdell out of the command.

At this point Sleeper repeated the "cowardly son-of-a-bitch" quotation and added a little more detail to the Bigelow conversation:

[Bigelow said] that Col. Blaisdell had gone up to II Corps Headquarters for the purpose of seeing Gen. Hancock to get the order breaking up the Old Division revoked. He further stated that Genl. Carr was not a Brigadier General, only Acting and that the Senate had refused to confirm the appointment.

The next witness was Sergeant Major William S. Rockhill, who wore the uniform of an acting first lieutenant, Company I, 11th New Jersey. Blake's objection to his attire was rejected. Rockhill quoted Bigelow as saying that General Carr was a "God-damned cowardly-son-of-a-bitch and a damned rascal, from the first Bull Run fight to the present time and that he could prove it." Blake asked Rockhill, "Has any promise been made to you that for your testimony here in this trial you would be mustered before Lieutenant Morehouse?" The judge advocate was quick to object, saying the question went to the veracity of the witness and that this could only be shown by testimony of his general reputation for truthfulness. The court upheld the objection.

Undismayed, Blake asked Rockhill, "How many times have you talked with General Carr about the testimony you have to give?" Judge Advocate Bingham again objected, saying the question was irrelevant in that Carr's motives were not the question before the court. The defense counsel's long losing record on objections remained intact, and the question was not allowed. The prosecution then rested.

Colonel Blaisdell was called as a defense witness. Blake asked him what report had Captain Bigelow made to him about the meeting. The colonel answered:

> He reported that the proceedings were harmonious and showed that the men were devoted to the cause, and the resolutions that he showed me I took them to be very patriotic. Everything was harmonious except a personal altercation between General Carr's brother that some hard words passed between them.

The younger brother, Lieutenant James H. Carr, was a member of the delegation from the 11th New Jersey at the meeting. Judge Advocate Bingham, on a cross examination he may have regretted, repeated the question as to whether Bigelow had reported on the remarks made by Forrest at the meeting. Colonel Blaisdell replied:

> He simply made the general remark that everything passed off harmoniously except that a drunken man, General Carr's brother, came in and with whom he had an altercation.

Blake was able to bring out that Captain Bigelow had been appointed inspector general of the brigade by General French and had served in that position while McAllister was in command. Later, as inspector general under Blaisdell, Bigelow must have questioned the activities of some of the other regimental commanders in addition to Merriam of the 16th Massachusetts. Apparently one of those under scrutiny was McAllister, who was asked about the assignment of General Carr's brother to the 11th New Jersey.

My Brother's Keeper

Somewhat mysteriously, Private James H. Carr of the 34th Massachusetts, who had been in the army since July 1862, was discharged by a special order of January 18, 1864, "to enable him to accept a commission in the same regiment." This was unlikely, since a few months previously Carr had been court martialled for being AWOL from the 34th Massachusetts. Actually, Carr got a commission in the 11th New Jersey which was delivered to his elder brother in early January 1864. On January 22, 1864, Blaisdell asked McAllister to explain "with the least possible delay" by what authority the younger Carr was assigned to the 11th New Jersey. "You will also state whether Lieutenant Carr was ever mustered as a first lieutenant in your regiment, if so, by whom mustered, by what authority, and into what company, and also if, at this time of said muster, there was a vacancy for a first lieutenant in that company, in accordance with existing orders."(105)

There is an entry on the muster roll for January 18 for Carr's appointment to the 11th New Jersey, but a later entry indicates he had been appointed on March 8, 1864. Perhaps questioning the validity of Lieutenant Carr's appointment was one of Blaisdell's earlier mentioned acts of "tyranny" toward General Carr and Colonel McAllister.

What the younger Carr did between January and March is not very clear. In March, however, he was put on detached service as an aide-de-camp to his brother, and he continued as such to the end of the war, although he was assigned to the 11th New Jersey the whole time. In his file is a letter from Lieutenant Colonel John Schoonover, then in command of the 11th New Jersey, dated April 1865, inquiring as to his status. Carr replied that he was still an aide to his brother at that time.

A final, somewhat bizarre, event in the saga is the forwarding of "charges and specifications" against Carr by Captain Rufus White of the 11th Massachusetts. The charges were basically the same as those for the other officers taking part in the protest meeting. In particular he was accused of declaring that "it is a shame to break-up the old Brigade," and thereby expressing his condemnation for his superior officers in the reorganization of the III Corps. The suggested witnesses for the prosecution were his fellow officers in the 11th New Jersey. The charges were forwarded through Colonel Blaisdell and Colonel Brewster to General Carr on April 11, at the height of the courts martial. Apparently General Carr did not appreciate the humor of the action and the charges went no further.

Blake observed that one of the problems of the military justice system was that:

Charges of a serious character must be approved by a general officer, who deliberately suppress them without any regard to the just interests of the service, if the culprit is one of his friends, or can repay him for his sinful kindness. Specifications that were filed against the brother of a division commander for habitual drunkenness never emerged from their hiding place when they reached his headquarters.(106)

The Defense Witnesses

In contrast to the prosecution witnesses, the defense witnesses came from all of the regiments that had been represented at the protest meeting:

Captain William C. Allen, Company G, 11th Massachusetts
Captain John S. Farley, Company F, 84th Pennsylvania
Captain Thomas O'Hare, Company G, 16th Massachusetts
Captain Charles C. Rivers, Company A, 11th Massachusetts
Captain Richard F. Lombard, Company F, 16th Massachusetts
First Lieutenant John H. Smith, Company I, 11th New Jersey
Adjutant William Teaffle, 11th Massachusetts
First Lieutenant Levi S. Russell, Company F, 11th Massachusetts
First Lieutenant Henry Jacques, Company G, 26th Pennsylvania

The other defendants were also defense witnesses, except for the excluded Henry Blake. If the prosecutors were after "active" as opposed to "passive" protesters, there were few "actives" on the defense witness list. Captain Lombard of the 16th Massachusetts served on the committee that drafted the resolution, and Lieutenant Smith of the 11th New Jersey seconded Forrest's motion of acceptance. The prosecution may have felt that pressing charges against these officers would dilute the impression that the meeting was an 11th Massachusetts operation.

The testimony of the defense witnesses was as uniform as that of the prosecution witnesses. They neither heard nor recalled any discussion at the meeting concerning the alteration or breaking up of either the corps or the division. They said that the focus of the meeting was on the breakup of the First Brigade. A number of them testified that DuPaget's speech opposing the motion was rambling and incoherent and generally created amusement among the audience. Lieutenant Russell suggested that he be given a "certificate" that he had voted against the motion. This suggestion raised a chorus of laughter. Some testified that Bigelow did not vote for the motion, while others just had no recollection of the matter. None of the witnesses heard Bigelow call General

Defense Witnesses

MOLLUS-USAMHI
Capt. William C. Allen, Co. G., 11th Mass., refused to chair the meeting.

MOLLUS-USMHI
Adj. Lt. William Teaffle, 11th Massachusetts.

MOLLUS-USAMHI
11th Mass. co. commanders (l to r) Capt. William Munroe, Co. K.; Capt. Charles C. Rivers, Co. A, a witness for the defense and a future colonel of the regiment; and Capt. Rufus White, who preferred charges against Gen. Carr's brother.

Carr a cowardly son-of-a-bitch. Somewhat surprisingly, Judge Advocate Bingham conducted little cross examination of the defense witnesses.

After Colonel Blaisdell's testimony, reported earlier, the defense rested. The judge advocate submitted the case to the court without remarks.

In the appendix of the original case file, written in Henry Blake's hand, is a brief of legal arguments for Captain Bigelow. One of the points made may not have helped Bigelow's cause:

> If the court is satisfied that I called Gen. Carr a coward and a rascal, I desire to say that he is so called by nine-tenths of the officers and enlisted men of the old First Brigade, Second Division, III Corps. He commanded my brigade nearly a year and a half and his reputation in these respects is established. Although I could not in this trial introduce evidence to prove my assertions true in point of fact, I shall feel satisfied if this defense should cause an investigation.

On the afternoon of April 6, 1864, the court found Captain Bigelow not guilty on the charge of mutiny, but guilty on the charge of "contemptuous and disrespectful conduct to his superior officer." He was sentenced to be cashiered.

After the war, Blake commented on the punishment:

> [C]ommon sense should be appealed to in fixing punishment by a Court Martial where there is discretion, and an officer who fights, fights, fights, should be kept in the service unless his offense is rank and smells to heaven.(107)

On the evening before Captain Bigelow was convicted, General Hays wrote to his wife,

> The court martial, of which I am president, is attracting attention, and I have no doubts would interest the public if the proceedings were published, which will be the case after the close of the trials.(108)

The Trial of Lieutenant Henry N. Blake

Henry Blake's trial opened on April 7. General Hays was not present for this proceeding, nor those of the three officers whose trials were still to come. It appears that Hays had tired of Blake's objections and exceptions and believed that he could better use his time in preparing his new brigade for battle. On April 9th he wrote to his wife:

> I have been relieved from the court-martial, but am hourly occupied in drilling and equipping my "rebellion crushers" for the coming campaign. I tried one tedious case in the court and set the machine going. I then applied to be relieved that I might devote my time to my brigade. . . . I am satisfied that our division is more proficient in exercise than any other in the army, east or west, but my own command shall be perfect, if I can make it so.
>
> I have many recruits, and they must be drilled and disciplined thoroughly.(109)

Colonel William R. Brewster of the New York Excelsior, the commander of the brigade that contained the 11th Massachusetts, became the presiding officer.

Blake, as had Bigelow, objected to Lieutenant Colonel Merriam serving on the court, although his reasons were a little more inflammatory than Bigelow's. In a legal memorandum included in the appendix of the case, he argued that

> [Merriam] has had many interviews with Brig. General Carr . . . and talked about the evidence and all the facts. . . . Upon one of these occasions said Gen. Carr uttered in the presence of said Lt. Col. Merriam these words: "I will follow up old Blaisdell and every officer from his staff until I get them out of the service. I have got Bigelow and Blake in a tight place and it will go hard with them," or words to that effect, and that said Lt. Col. Merriam heard this remark and acquiesced in the same.
>
> 2nd. The said Lt. Col. Waldo Merriam stated in the hearing of the officers of his regiment . . . when summonses of this honorable Court were delivered to said officers of his regiment to appear as witnesses in the case of Capt. Bigelow: "I hope every officer of any regiment who goes to that Court-Martial to testify in Capt. Bigelow's case will be

court-martialled for the same offense and be convicted," or words to that effect.

To back up his allegations, Blake listed as potential witnesses General Carr, six members of his staff and six members of Merriam's staff. Merriam asked to be excused "because from a conversation with the colonel of the 11th Massachusetts I have learned that there exists an idea in his regiment that I have been implicated in the charges preferred against the accused."

The charges against Blake were the same as those for all of the cases other than Bigelow—"insubordinate conduct to the prejudice of good order and military discipline." The first specification was that Blake "did take part and assist" in the protest meeting and "did permit" a motion to be made that a "committee of three be appointed to draft resolutions to express the disgust of the Division with the contemplated alterations of the III Corps." The second specification was that Blake had acted as secretary of the meeting "for purposes of expressing condemnation or censure of their superior officers for their actions in the reorganization of lately composing the III Corps."

The lead-off prosecution witness again was Alfred DuPaget. The judge advocate followed his earlier pattern of questioning as to the object of the meeting. Blake, acting as his own counsel, again maintained that the best evidence for this were the minutes of the meeting and resolutions adopted. The judge advocate argued that the testimony of Lieutenant DuPaget would bring out the sentiments of the meeting prior to the adoption of the resolution which were not brought out in the minutes.

The court allowed the question and DuPaget stated that George Forrest had said it "was to express the disgust of the officers of the Second Division with the contemplated alteration in the III Corps . . . with great emphasis used on the word 'disgust'." DuPaget was then asked by Bingham whether there was any opposition to the resolution. Blake posed a more general objection, stating that the "prosecution must show a connection between the accused and Quartermaster Forrest, that what one said necessarily expressed the sentiments of the other."

The judge advocate maintained that his line of questioning would bring out those who actively supported the resolution after its object was clear. Captain Bingham was still struggling with the mild content of the resolution:

The object of the question is to show that certain statements—on the part of certain parties present—possibly necessitated the conservative views expressed in the resolutions.

The court admitted the question and DuPaget answered that he was the only officer at the meeting who had voted against the resolution and had made a speech indicating that it, in his words, "was contrary to good order and military discipline and we were all liable to be court martialled for it and that it was 'treason' to the Commander-in-Chief of the Army and the President of the United States."

On cross examination, Blake asked DuPaget whether "it was usual for recording officers of meetings like this one to take part in the discussion or vote upon the motion." He replied that he had never been to a military meeting which had a secretary and president.

The judge advocate called William S. Rockhill, and his testimony of the earlier trial was repeated, as were Blake's objections. Blake asked him on cross examination if the remarks of Lieutenant DuPaget were "treated in a light manner, and made the subject of joke and ridicule by many officers." Rockhill answered, "By many officers, no, sir."

Captain Sleeper testified as in the Bigelow case, emphasizing the use by Forrest of the phrase "utter disgust" in the condemnation of the reorganization. On cross examination, Sleeper was asked whether DuPaget's remarks were very mumbling and incoherent. He answered, "I thought they were very much to the point." Blake's final question to Sleeper was, "Why did you remain silent and offer no opposition?" Sleeper answered, "I did not wish to have anything to do with the meeting until I knew exactly its object. As soon as the character of the meeting had developed itself, I left." The prosecution then closed its case.

Blake called Captain Bigelow as his first defense witness and asked what order or message he had given to Blake prior to the meeting. Bigelow replied:

I told him that it was the Colonel's order that there were to be no altercations or drunkenness in the Hall and that he was to assist me if necessary.

Blake then asked Bigelow why he, Blake, had been appointed secretary. The captain responded, "the lieutenant has generally acted as secretary in several of the meetings in the regiment and brigade." After the war, Blake wrote, "I was chosen Secretary and like a chump accepted."(110)

Blake then proposed to introduce evidence "that affected the veracity and reputation of one of the witnesses for the prosecution." Judge Advocate Bingham objected to the introduction of any testimony that would either directly or indirectly impeach the veracity of Lieutenant DuPaget except by disproving the facts stated by him or going to his general reputation for truthfulness. The motion to introduce such evidence was denied.

Blake then tried a slightly different approach. He asked Bigelow, "Have you any means of knowledge as to whether or not Lieutenant DuPaget is a man of truth and veracity?" Captain Bigelow responded:

I have seen a document from him to the Headquarters of the division and the endorsement of the officers upon its return to Brigade headquarters. Sometime within two months DuPaget complained that he had lost his eye-sight to such a degree as to disqualify him from doing picket duty. A question arose and a commission of three surgeons were appointed to examine this case. They reported that the complaint was groundless— that it was not so.

Lieutenant DuPaget then took exception in writing addressed to the Medical Director of the Division. Dr. [J. F.] Calhoun returned it endorsed that he was personally acquainted with the three surgeons and that their reputation for veracity and skill were too well established to admit of any doubt as to their decision, and recommended that Lieutenant Du-Paget be arrested and tried by court martial for malingering.

On cross examination by the judge advocate, Bigelow admitted that he had not seen the document written by DuPaget stating that he had lost his eyesight such as to disqualify him from duty. The court asked Bigelow, "Would you not think that Lieutenant DuPaget erred in judgement rather than intended falseness relating to his fitness for duty?" The captain answered, "I do not know the officer. I never had a moment's conversation with him other than officially."

The judge advocate asked if he would believe the testimony of DuPaget on oath. "No, sir, for I heard him testify in my own case to two lies," Bigelow responded.

The other officers then testified. Forrest, on being asked, "Did you make any remarks other than the simple motion to draft a resolution as they deem proper?" inexplicably took the fifth amendment. He was then asked, "Did you state the object of the meeting other than in words stated in your motion?" He answered in the negative. In later questioning, Forrest maintained he had used the word "regret" rather than "disgust" in discussing the break-up of the brigade.

Captain Lombard of the 16th Massachusetts testified for the defense that the words of Lieutenant DuPaget were taken lightly and had not influenced the committee who had drawn up the resolutions. Captain William Munroe testified that he had known Henry Blake for three years and that he had been a good lieutenant in Company K.

The court found Blake not guilty of insubordinate conduct but guilty of conduct to the prejudice of good order and military discipline. The penalty was forfeiture of three months pay and allowances and to be reprimanded in General Orders. The court said that the imposition of such a mild punishment was due to the fourteen days of close confinement the accused had already served.

The following is Blake's summary of his arrest and court martial:

An episode occurred in my military career, which may not be of general interest; but an omission to allude to it might produce a slight degree of surprise and criticism. I was detailed to act as judge-advocate of a court martial in the morning, placed under arrest in the afternoon, and transported with four officers in a wagon which was marked very conspicuously "Provost Guard," and followed by a detachment of soldiers to the headquarters of the corps. I was closely confined three weeks in a log shelter in which there were no windows, but the rents in the roof admitted light. No friends were allowed to the quarters unless the corps commander granted permission; and sentinels constantly paced their beats at all hours, and watched the prison, because I had acted as secretary of an orderly meeting of officers that adopted resolutions of the highest loyalty and patriotism, which were duly transmitted to Gen. Meade and the Chairman of the War Committee of Congress. The perjury of three unscrupulous witnesses complicated the case; and, while some were dismissed from service, a heavy fine was imposed upon the author and subsequently remitted by the commander of the corps, who was convinced of the utter injustice.(111)

Blake wrote that three witnesses committed perjury, but four witnesses testified. Captain Sleeper had the least to gain materially from cooperating with the prosecution, although he was a close friend of Colonel McAllister. Blake later accused him, saying:

We supposed we were a secret consultation of friends, but we were betrayed by a Judas in the person of Captain Sleeper of the 11th New Jersey.(112)

The two sergeants who were acting lieutenants, Rockhill and Morehouse, would have benefited from the approval of Colonel McAllister in their quest to be mustered as officers. And they both had been close to McAllister, if not General Carr.

Whether or not he acknowledged it at the time, Blake later admitted:

There was no hope for an escape, and the measurement of punishment was practically the sole question for decision. . . . I offered to prove by three hundred witnesses that Gen. Carr was a coward and dishonest, but this testimony was rejected properly, because a soldier has no right to utter a word against an officer unless he is called as a witness in a judicial tribunal, or submits a report to a department of the government in the performance of his duty. The truth or falsehood of what was said by Capt. Bigelow was not inquired into or adjudged. I concede the defendants were convicted in accordance with the regulations and rules governing the Army.(113)

Col. Blaisdell conferred most confidentially with me after I returned to duty and told me he had seen Gen. Hancock, and denounced my sentence as a d–d outrage, and asked that the fine be remitted; he told him I was one of the most reliable officers in the Regiment always sober and ready for duty. Gen. Hancock said Gen. Meade was jealous of his position as Commander of the II Corps and thought he might be removed on some pretext, "but after I [Hancock] have fought in one battle of this campaign I shall be secure. But you tell Lieutenant Blake to go on and do his duty, and the first chance I have I will remit the penalties against him." This is the substance of conversation between me and Col. Blaisdell. . . . I do not entertain any doubt the interviews between Gen. Hancock and Col. Blaisdell were reported to me correctly, including the revelation of the relations between two generals of high rank, like Meade and Hancock.(114)

Blake ran into Hancock himself a few years after the war, and he gave credence to Blaisdell's account.

Gen. Hancock was in Virginia City, Montana, in 1868, on an inspection tour as commander of the military district embracing Montana, and I called on him and reviewed battle scenes, and he entertained the visitors with stories of my Commander, Col. Blaisdell, and how he got his name, Old Cruelty, by being very strict in his discipline. I referred to my Court Martial and he declared the sentence was unjust.(115)

All this did not impress the Treasury Department's second auditor who, twenty years later and after General Hancock had died, declared that Blake owed the government his $300 fine. It appears that neither Blake nor Smith had paid, but the innocent victim, Thomas of the 26th Pennsylvania, had had his fine deducted from his pay.(116)

The Trial of Captain Walter N. Smith

Captain Walter N. Smith, Company B, 11th Massachusetts, was tried on April 12 and 15, the court martial being unable to muster a quorum on the 14th. The specifications were that he had supported and voted for the protest motion and had said that "he would take the resolutions proposed to be drafted to express the disgust of the Division upon the contemplated alterations in the Corps around, and get them signed by officers of the Brigade, and those who refused to sign them could go to Hell, or words to that effect."

Alfred DuPaget repeated his testimony, and further stated that Captain Smith, after his speech of opposition, had declared that "the door was open and the gentlemen who had previously spoken, meaning me, or anybody else who were opposed to

MOLLUS-USAMHI
Defendant Capt. Walter N. Smith, 11th Mass., was outspoken and profane, but had political clout to fall back on.

proceeding had better go to their quarters."

Captain Sleeper played a smaller role in this trial since he had left the meeting before Smith allegedly made his statement. Sleeper did say that the accused frequently used "profane and vile expressions."

Sergeant Rockhill was called over Blake's usual objection, which was now denied on the growing number of precedents of *US v. Bigelow* and *US v. Blake*. His only new testimony was that Captain Smith had said something against part of the resolution about obeying the orders "of such officers as were put in command over us provided we saw fit." Rockhill did not say whether the statement was made before or after the resolutions were adopted.

DuPaget was recalled by the judge advocate over Blake's objection. He testified that he was instructed by the Lt. Col. Commanding the Regiment [Schoonover] to go in person to the officers of the Regiment and inform them that he had heard that the meeting to be held that night was an indignation meeting and that it was his advice to them not to go there and be careful of what part they took in the proceedings.

John W. Kuhl Collection
Capt. John Sowter, Co. B, 11th NJ, testified as a defense witness. He was dismissed from the army three months later for misconduct at Spotsylvania.

While carrying out this instruction, he met Captain Smith of the 11th Massachusetts in the quarters of Lieutenant Smith of the 11th New Jersey.

Blake came up with a new witness from the 11th New Jersey, one who was not following the regimental line. Captain John Sowter, Company B, testified that DuPaget's remarks "created a good deal of laughter and amusement for the whole meeting," as did the suggestion that he be given a "certificate" for his vote in opposition. Sowter testified that he did not hear discussion about breaking up the III Corps or the division or expressions of condemnation of superior officers. He said he did not hear Captain Smith use the expression "hell" or "devil," and stated that he did not hear Smith make a remark about obeying superior officers "as we saw fit."

The testimony of First Lieutenant J. Heilig, Company D, 26th Pennsylvania, was very similar to that of Captain Sowter's. He said the discussion was solely about breaking up the brigade and he thought that Lieutenant Forrest had modified his motion to substitute the word "regret" for the word "disgust." First Lieutenant Henry Jacques, Company G, 26th Pennsylvania, testified for the defense with similar answers. He stated in summary:

> The reason the whole Division was not there was because the Commander of the Brigade I now belong to ordered his officers to stay away. We had no orders to stay away. There was nothing done disloyal, no superior's names used in the meeting in any way, shape or manner. The whole and full object of the meeting was expressed in the Resolution.

Like Blake, Captain Smith was found not guilty of insubordination but guilty of "conduct to the prejudice of good order and military discipline." His punishment was the same as Blake's.

A look at Smith's background offers a hint of why he may have been on the prosecution's hit list. Before the war Smith was a machinist from Lowell, Massachusetts, and was an original member of Company B, the Paul Revere Guard. He was promoted from sergeant to first lieutenant after First Bull Run and became captain of Company B just before the Peninsula campaign. He was injured at Harrison's landing when he and his horse fell into a well.

The previous summer, at about the same time that General Carr was court martialling Henry Blake, Captain Smith had made a comment on the state of the Army of the Potomac and its leadership that had gotten him into big trouble. On July 29, 1863, Carr brought charges against Smith for "uttering treasonable language" while on the march from Salem to Warrenton, Virginia. The language "made in the presence of officers and enlisted men of his regiment" was alleged to be "God damn the service. I hope to Jesus Christ that Jeff Davis will lick us in every fight we go into," or words to that effect.

The second charge of "disrespect to his superior officers" was based on the tendering of his resignation "for the following reason—not wishing to serve under the present commanders of the Army of the Potomac."

Captain Smith did not have much of a defense, and Blake did not participate. The latter appears to have decided it might be unwise to appear before General Carr since his own court martial had taken place only three weeks earlier. The presiding officer of the court was the commanding officer of the 11th

Massachusetts, Lieutenant Colonel Porter Tripp. Smith was found guilty and his sentence was that "he be dismissed from the service [and] forever after be debarred from holding any position of pay or trust under the United States Government."

What Smith lacked in his defense on the merits, he more than made up for in terms of political influence. His file includes a letter from a Maine political figure whose signature cannot be made out, and a note from Vice President Hannibal Hamlin to President Lincoln requesting "suspension of action" on the court martial conviction. The Maine politician, a friend of Smith's father, wrote that

Captain Smith left a good situation to enlist as a private, from purely patriotic feelings, having a wife and children. He rose by distinguished merit and service to be a Captain, and is the best officer in his regiment. He probably expressed his disgust at official stupidity of some toad-eater who don't like gunpowder. A letter from General Sickles, here before me, speaks of Capt. Smith as "an officer of distinguished merit."

It appears that before this correspondence had reached Warrenton, the Second Division Commander, General Prince, had already disapproved the conviction on the first charge, in that the "degrading language" was made "under circumstances which forbade it being taken or meant in its treasonable signification." He suggested a penalty of the loss of two month's pay. The final disposition of the case was made by General Meade, when apparently all the communications were in his hand on September 14:

The division commander has disapproved the finding on the first charge. The sentence is based upon findings on both the charges and under the circumstances must fall. Capt. Walter N. Smith, 11th Massachusetts, will be released from arrest and will return today.

So much for treason and the actions of toad-eaters.

The Trial of Lieutenant George Forrest

After a few false starts, the trial of the quartermaster, George Forrest, opened on April 21 and progressed in the repetitive fashion of the previous trials. The prosecution objected to Blake as counsel and Blake objected to Merriam on the court. Blake won both of these points.

One of the specifications against Forrest was that he had organized the meeting, and there was testimony from Quartermaster Sergeant Bernard Colly that Forrest had given him notices of the meeting which he was ordered to deliver to the adjutants of the Hooker Brigade regiments.

There followed the usual prosecution witnesses from the 11th New Jersey, including Sergeant Morehouse, who had not been used since the Bigelow trial. Captain Sleeper testified that after DuPaget's speech, Forrest had said that "he was willing to sign his name to such resolution in as large characters as possible." Sergeant Rockhill was cross examined by Blake to suggest, as was done in previous trials, that he was not at the meeting. Blake asked why he had omitted references to the "certificate" incident. He stated he was not certain whether such remarks were made or were not made. Blake then asked Rockhill, "Who informed General Carr about the proceedings of said meeting?" Judge Advocate Bingham objected immediately, and the question was withdrawn.

The court adjourned until April 23, when the prosecution recalled Lieutenant DuPaget. The judge advocate had apparently failed to get testimony that Lieutenant Forrest had voted for his motion. DuPaget obliged and the prosecution rested.

The first defense witness, who would be considered hostile, was Lieutenant Colonel Schoonover. As previously noted, he testified about the group who had met in Colonel McAllister's quarters and had

MOLLUS-USAMHI
Defendant George Forrest, a first lieutenant, was quartermaster of the 11th Massachusetts.

decided to send a report on the meeting to General Carr.

The defense witnesses were: captains John S. Farley and Charles C. Rivers from the 11th Massachusetts, Captain Sowter from the 11th New Jersey, and Captain Otis Hoyt, Company B, 16th Massachusetts. They generally stated that the resolutions adopted expressed the object of the meeting and that DuPaget's speech had not affected their content. There was also quite a lot of testimony concerning Forrest's use of the word "disgust" and his substitution of the word "regret." None of the witnesses saw or heard Forrest vote for the resolution. Some of these witnesses estimated that there were fifty or sixty officers at the meeting, considerably higher than the estimates in the earlier trials.

Captain Bigelow appeared as a witness and was questioned as to whether DuPaget's testimony in his trial was at odds with his testimony in the current trial. The judge advocate objected on the ground that Blake was trying to impeach the witness in an incorrect manner. The question was not allowed, and Blake asked Bigelow, "from the testimony of DuPaget in your trial and his reputation in general, would you believe him under oath?" A negative answer was elicited.

The defense rested. The court found Lieutenant Forrest guilty on the charges and specifications. The sentence was that he "be dismissed from the service of the United States."

The Trial of Captain Edward C. Thomas

On April 26 the last of the officers, Captain Edward C. Thomas, 26th Pennsylvania, came to trial. The only defendant who did not belong to the 11th Massachusetts, his offense was that he was the presiding officer at the meeting. His trial was quite *pro forma* compared to the prior ones. Colonel McAllister had earlier characterized Captain Thomas as an innocent victim.(117) DuPaget testified that Thomas only served "as an act of kindness" to his fellow officers. Sergeant Rockhill was of the opinion that "he was induced to serve that the proposed resolution might be of a milder or more conservative nature." Captain Thomas testified that he had never before in his whole life presided at a meeting. It is unlikely he would ever again accept such a position. Two new defense witnesses called by Blake were lieutenants John H. Smith, Company I, 11th New Jersey and Thomas J. Morris, Company G, 26th Pennsylvania.

Captain Thomas was sentenced to the same fine and reprimand given to Captain Smith and Lieutenant Blake.

The Brandy Station courts martial was declared dissolved by a special order of May 4, 1864. The II Corps had already started marching for the Rapidan crossings on their way to the Wilderness.

During the period of the courts martial, Henry Blake, who was not particularly interested in military advancement, was promoted to captain, ironically filling the vacancy created by Captain Bigelow's departure.(118)

General Hancock in the Middle

Winfield Scott Hancock, upon his assignment to the new II Corps, was confronted with the charges brought by General Carr, the result of III Corps politics. Initially he appeared to support his newly appointed division commander, whose integrity and courage were being attacked, but Carr's nomination for appointment, which was looking more and more questionable on the eve of the spring campaign, was the work of generals Meade and Humphreys, not of Hancock.

The relationship between General Hancock and the old III Corps divisions, brigades and regiments was somewhat ambivalent. Captain Blake did not write disapprovingly of General Hancock, as he did of Meade, although his praise was generally reserved for Generals Hooker and Kearny, and Sickles, to a lesser extent. Blake's only criticism of General Hancock was not personal but based on the fact that he had gotten undue credit for his part in the battle of Williamsburg where McClellan first referred to him as "superb".(119)

These old tensions did not die easily. General Regis DeTrobriand, the commander of the First Brigade, Third Division, of the new II Corps, wrote of a conversation in General Hancock's tent in October of 1864, right before the election. He noted that Hancock "leaned very near the Democratic party, but had not endorsed either Lincoln or McClellan, desiring to run with the hare and hold with the hounds.'" DeTrobriand recalled the incident:

Unfortunately, I commented with some force on the consideration due General McClellan as a statesman and as a soldier. I was treading there on delicate ground. I passed along rapidly, and, taking up the Peninsular

MOLLUS-USAMHI

Gen. Regis DeTrobriand was the commander of the Third Brigade, First Division, of III Corps. Later in 1864 he led the First Brigade, Third Division, II Corps.

campaign, I quickly touched on the battle of Williamsburg. Carried away by too great confidence in the liberality of the general, and in his impartiality as to well known facts, I recalled Hooker, abandoned during the whole morning without support; the general-in-chief remaining behind in Yorktown; his arrival in the evening, when everything was over; his ignorance of what had happened—alas! and the famous dispatch wherein mention was made of Hancock, without a word about Hooker, Kearny or [John James] Peck.

"Not that I intend for a moment to underrate in the least the importance of your part in the battle," I added, addressing myself to Hancock, plainly annoyed. "In that respect there can be but one voice, and, as much as any one can, I appreciate how much your brilliant action on that occasion did you honor. But I appeal to yourself: what can be thought of a general-in-chief capable of such conduct, and of injustice towards three generals out of four?"

I must acknowledge, the peroration failed to have any effect. The fourth general was little affected by the fact that I recognized the justice of his treatment, as soon as I spoke of the injustice of which the others had been the victims. I had touched a sore spot; the oil I poured upon it did not allay the irritation.

"I understand," said General Hancock, breaking up the session, "You are all alike in the old III Corps. In your eyes, you have done everything in this war, and all others nothing."

I protested in vain; wounded vanity does not reason. I saw plainly that, by a few words too freely spoken, I had not only lost the goodwill of my corps commander, but had also revived his prejudice against the whole Third Division.(120)

In his report on the battle of Boydton Plank Road which immediately followed the ill fated discussion, Hancock gave, in DeTrobriand's words, "a lesson in modesty to those of the old III Corps, who believed they had always done everything."(121) Hancock gave the Second Division the bulk of the credit and deemphasized the Third Division's role. One fact was certain, DeTrobriand wrote, "the Second Division did not lose half as many men as the Third."(122) Fortunately for DeTrobriand's military career, this was General Hancock's last battle as Commander of the II Corps.

The Aftermath of the Reorganization and Courts Martial

Generals Alexander Hays and Gershom Mott both questioned Meade's decision to appoint Carr as commander of the new Fourth Division. On April 30th, Meade wrote to secretary of war Edwin M. Stanton that "this is producing disquiet and bad feeling, and I desire, if possible, to have [it] settled one way or the other before the army moves."(123)

In a day or so it was settled and Carr was out, ordered to report to General Benjamin Butler, who was commander of the Union forces operating between the York and James rivers. General Mott replaced Carr as commander of the Fourth Division and Colonel McAllister replaced Mott as commander of the First Brigade. Blake's suggestion of General Hays, with his III Corps background, for command of the Fourth Division had real merit. It might have been a real shot in the arm to the Fourth, although, as the Garibaldi Guards had said when Hays was rumored to be their new commander, he "might have gotten them all killed."(124)

As it turned out, the Fourth Division lasted less than a month. In a sense it became the scapegoat for the II Corps problems in the battles of the Wilderness and Spotsylvania. Typical of the commentary on its performance would be that of Lieutenant Colonel Theodore Lyman:

Mott's division [at the Wilderness] behaved badly (as you observed, it broke and came back). This is a curious instance of a change of morale. It is Hooker's old fighting division, but has since been under two

81

commanders of little merit or force of character; then there was some discontent about reenlistments and about breaking up of the old III Corps, to which it had belonged; and the result has been that most of this once crack division has conducted itself most discreditably, this campaign.(125)

And after Spotsylvania:

May 16. Mott's division, that had hitherto behaved so badly, was broken up and put with Birney—a sad record for Hooker's fighting men! Napoleon said that food, clothing, discipline and arms were one quarter, and morale the other three quarters.(126)

This may be too harsh a characterization of the performance of the Fourth; there was plenty of blame to go around in the Army of the Potomac after the Wilderness and Spotsylvania. But the fact that between thirty and fifty company level officers of five regiments had expressed their displeasure with the dismantling of the Hooker Brigade, and that the II Corps had court martialled five of them and implicitly threatened many more, could hardly have enhanced their fighting spirit. The fact that Colonel Brewster, the new Second Brigade Commander, was on the court martial board and that Colonel McAllister, the new First Brigade Commander, was highly sympathetic to the prosecution, might reasonably diminish these officers' favorable identification with their new units and leaders, and the II Corps generally.

The loss of Captain Bigelow and Lieutenant Forrest certainly did not help the 11th Massachusetts in the coming battles. Blake cites ammunition problems in the Wilderness that conceivably might have been avoided with an experienced quartermaster. And if Blaisdell was correct in his assessment of Bigelow's fighting qualities, an officer who could "rally troops" would have been very useful.

And many of the veterans had been worn down by three years of war and their experience in the last month might have further affected their fighting spirit. Colonel McAllister in his reports pointed to expiring enlistments as a primary cause for the performance problems of the Division. The last day or last month or last mission syndrome is a real one, but hard to measure and document.

It should be pointed out that despite the protest, a substantial number of the 11th Massachusetts' veteran officers and protest participants stayed on. These included Blaisdell, contrary to McAllister's prediction that he would go home when he lost command of the brigade. Others who stayed included defense witness Charles C. Rivers, who ultimately rose to colonel with command of the regiment, and captains Rufus A. White, Daniel Granger and Alexander McTavish. Lieutenant William Teaffle, another defense witness, reenlisted, as did Captain Richard Lombard, a member of the committee that drafted the protest resolution, who joined the 11th Massachusetts when the 16th Massachusetts was mustered out in July 1864. The 11th inherited the remaining men from both the 1st and 16th Massachusetts and was the only surviving regiment from the original Hooker Brigade.

In the chaos of battle that followed the courts martial, the angel of death hovered over the men who served on the board and those who participated in the trials. General Hays' characterization of the board's selection "for grit and fearlessness in discharge of duty" proved only too true. Within a period of a week, General Hays, Major Abbott and Captain Hamilton would be killed in the Wilderness, and Lieutenant Colonel Merriam would die at Spotsylvania. Other participants in the trial would not fare much better. The judge advocate, Captain Bingham, and defense counsel, Captain Blake, would both be seriously wounded at Spotsylvania, while the key prosecution witness, Captain Sleeper, and defense witness Lieutenant Morris, would be killed in that battle.

IV. The Reorganized Army is Tested

The Wilderness

When the Fourth Division broke camp shortly after the courts martial ended, Private Samuel Blood had been at Brandy Station for just a month. He probably had only the vaguest idea about the courts martial and the politics surrounding the demise of the Hooker Brigade. He had not been a soldier long enough to have morale to lose. Captain William Munroe's Company K morning report for April shows that Blood and three other recruits reported on April 3.(127) He and his buddies had probably received the rudimentary basic training, but it surely was not adequate for what the 11th Massachusetts was going to face in the next couple of days. The veterans from Boston, however, were not in much better shape for fighting in the Wilderness.

Letters written by both General Hays and Major Abbott indicate that the training of the Army of the Potomac was not particularly relevant to the fighting that was to go on in the Wilderness. Hays commanded the Second Brigade of General Birney's Third Division. On April 9, he wrote to his wife:

> I wish you could see our drills, or dress parades. The latter extends for a quarter of a mile in masses five divisions deep. All the field and staff officers are mounted. All the evolutions are much more imposing than any you have seen. Whether on drill or parade, at "officer's call" from the bugle, each officer commanding a battalion gallops to headquarters, so that my subordinates are always brought to within speaking distance at short notice.(128)

Private Blood may have seen some of these martial displays and marched in a big parade before his military career was abruptly terminated in battle. The

II Corps was reviewed on one of those days in mid April when the courts martial were in recess. In a letter to his mother, Major Abbott described the performance of his regiment, the 20th Massachusetts, which was in General Alexander Webb's First Brigade of General John Gibbon's Second Division.

Russell Blood

Private Samuel L. Blood of the 11th Mass. Volunteer Regiment, the author's grandfather, was wounded in the battle of the Wilderness.

We knocked all the other three divisions of the corps into pie. This regiment led the column, & with glittering brass, polished belts, shining faces, white gloves & trefoils to contrast, well set up, hair & beard close cut & clothes clean, but above all marching in lines absolutely perfect, the rear rank moving snug on the front rank and like Siamese twins, it could not be surpassed. All the generals were in raptures over the regiment. . . . Gibbon sent for me into his tent, where there were nothing but general officers, & I was presented to Meade & seven others, who all spoke in the most flattering manner of the 20th.(129)

But in battle the II Corps would march into a thicket of second growth trees and bushes that replaced a forest cut to supply fuel to the iron smelting furnaces established near Germanna Ford on the Rapidan by Alexander Spotswood, a colonial governor of Virginia, for whom Spotsylvania is named.(130)

Captain Blake described the Wilderness, which was no parade ground:

There were no commanding elevations or open tracts of ground upon which the artillery could be planted; and the firing was necessarily restricted to the small-arms, that slay the ten of thousands while the shells and shot destroy the thousands. The great contest occurred in midst of an almost impenetrable jungle of scrub oak, decayed trees, dense underbrush, and short pines, in which a regiment could not be discerned at the distance of a hundred feet; and the proper formation of the ranks seemed to be an impossibility. It was rarely intersected by public ways over which the infantry could move; and the pioneers were continually engaged in felling trees and cutting new roads to facilitate communication between the right and left. Packed mules, which transferred axes and shovels, were attached to every brigade, and formed an invaluable auxiliary during the campaign.(131)

The 11th Massachusetts on May 1st and 2nd had destroyed their winter huts at Brandy Station and were bivouacked in the fields so they could start on a moment's notice. The order to march came at 10:30 P.M. the night of the 3rd, and II Corps advanced to the Rapidan by the early hours of May 4th. Captain Blake wrote:

The veterans, that had made their footprints upon many lengthy and dreary roads, reserved their strength, and silently followed the file leaders; and verdant recruits and substitutes were the only babblers. The beginning of this campaign was like all those which had preceded it; and thousands of overcoats and blankets were scattered in the woods and fields through which the soldiers passed. The cavalry gained the commanding heights of the Rapidan without a contest; and the regiment crossed the river at Ely's Ford at half past twelve, P.M., upon a pontoon bridge that consisted of nine boats which had been anchored twenty-one feet apart.(132)

The Army of the Potomac's custom of abandoning blankets and overcoats on the first day of march was not appreciated by General Grant, who wrote that it was "an improvidence I had never witnessed before."(133)

The regiment marched rapidly for about three hours and at 3 P.M. halted for the night at the scene of the battle of Chancellorsville. If Private Blood had been one of the babblers, the surroundings of the first night's campsite may have had a sobering effect. Blake wrote:

Many of the Union dead had been exhumed, or remain unburied; jaws, arms and legs were bleaching upon the soil; and the wasps and moles made their nests in some of the skulls. Not a shot was fired during the day; no bugle or drum resounded through the forest; the unnatural

Library of Congress

II Corps crosses the Rapidan at Ely's Ford on May 4th in this sketch by noted Civil War artist Alfred Waud, who was on the scene. The pontoon bridge is mentioned in Henry Blake's record of the event.

stillness which precedes the dreadful tempest reigned; and the brigade bivouacked upon the same spot that it occupied on the same date of the previous year.(134)

The regiment was awakened at 3 A.M. on May 5th and after breakfast resumed its march. Under the operational plan worked up by generals Meade and Humphreys, the II Corps was to go to the right of the Confederate forces, while the V Corps under Gouverneur Warren and the VI Corps under John Sedgwick were to go to the Confederate left. More particularly, the V Corps was to move toward Parker's Store on the Plank Road, while the VI Corps was to move to the Wilderness Tavern area at the intersection of the Orange Turnpike and the road to Germanna Ford.(135)

Lieutenant Morris Schaff, general headquarters staff member and, in later years a historian of the battle of the Wilderness, explained the major roads:

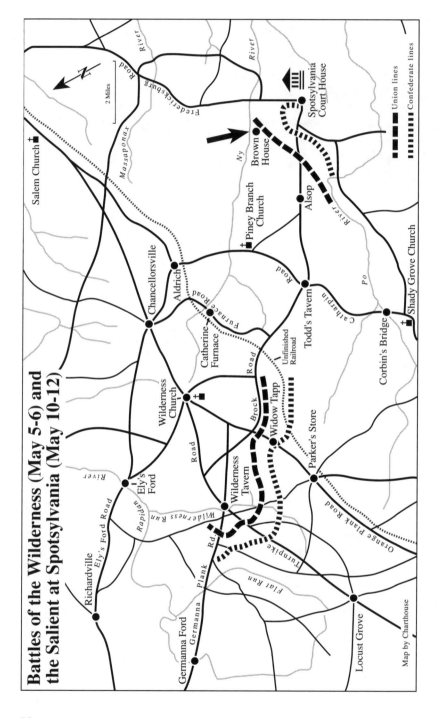

Battles of the Wilderness (May 5-6) and the Salient at Spotsylvania (May 10-12)

Map by Charthouse

Union lines
Confederate lines

Salem Church

Fredericksburg Road

Massaponax

2 Miles

River

River

Ny

Spotsylvania Court House

Brown House

Piney Branch Church

Alsop

River

Road

Po

Chancellorsville

Aldrich

Furnace Road

Todd's Tavern

Catharpin

Shady Grove Church

Catherine Furnace

Road

Corbin's Bridge

Unfinished Railroad

Wilderness Church

Brock

Widow Tapp

Parker's Store

Road

Ely's Ford

River

Wilderness Run

Wilderness Tavern

Ely's Ford Road

Rapidan

Orange Plank Road

Richardville

Flat Run

Plank Rd.

Turnpike

Germanna Ford

Germanna Plank Road

Locust Grove

88

Running through the Wilderness its entire length is what is known as the Fredericksburg and Orange Court House Turnpike, a famous post road in the old stage days. Leaving Fredericksburg, it bears almost due west till it reaches the heart of the Wilderness; there it crosses Wilderness Run, and then, diverting its course slightly to the south of west, aims straight for Orange Court House some eighteen miles away. At the time of the war the stage-day glory of the road and its old taverns, Dowdall's at Chancellorsville, the Wilderness overlooking the run of the same name, Robertson's at Locust Grove, were all gone; most of the stables and some of the houses were mere ruins, and the roadbed itself lapsed into that of a common earth road. When the system of plank roads came into vogue, about 1845, one was built a few miles south of, but more or less paralleling, the Turnpike. It is known as the Orange and Fredericksburg Plank Road, and at the time of the battle was in about the same forlorn state as its rival, the Pike.(136)

The First Day

The II Corps objective for the day was the Shady Grove Church, at the intersection of the Pamunkey and Catharpin roads. The line of march for the II Corps was past the ruins of the Chancellorsville House, turn right on Catherine Furnace Road, turn left on Brock Road, and then right on Catharpin Road at Todd's Tavern. When Gibbon's Division, the lead unit, had reached a point about a mile down Catharpin Road at about 9:00 A.M., a message (sent at 7:30) was received by General Hancock ordering him to hold in place. It had been recognized by the high command that General Robert E. Lee was not behaving in the way that had been anticipated. Meade and Humphreys believed that Lee would not fight in the Wilderness but possibly in the Mine Run area as he had done in the previous November. But now Lee (A. P. Hill's III Corps) appeared to be coming right up Orange Plank Road, engaging Union calvary at Parker's Store, and endangering Warren's flank. Moreover, the Confederate II Corps (Richard S. Ewell) was on the Orange Turnpike and apparently threatening Charles Griffin's Division of the V Corps.

At 9 A.M. on May 5th, the II Corps divisions were spread out over about six miles of narrow roads: Gibbon's had just turned on Catharpin Road, Birney was on Brock Road, and Mott and Francis C. Barlow were on Furnace Road. For about two hours Meade attempted to sort out the situation. Grant was just coming up from the Rapidan at the time. By 10 A.M. Meade was fairly convinced that A. P. Hill's III Corps meant business on Plank Road and threatened the crucial intersection with Brock Road. At about 10:30 A.M., Grant, now on the scene, called for a general attack down the Orange Turnpike and Culpeper Mine Road by the V and VI Corps. He also ordered General George Getty's Division, the lead division of the VI Corps, to proceed to the intersection of Plank and Brock roads, and then attack down Plank Road toward Parker's Store. The II Corps was to abandon its flanking action and support Getty.

Some knowledgeable commentators have questioned this decision. Francis Walker wrote:

> What would have been the result had Hancock, instead of being halted and subsequently recalled, been ordered to push with all his force into the enemy's rear. Only five out of nine of Lee's Divisions were up: might not the V and VI Corps have been trusted to hold these in check? The day was only fairly opened; the commander of the turning column was a resolute and energetic soldier; he had under him twenty-eight thousand men. A rapid movement into the rear of the forces opposing Warren would have raised a very interesting issue. Hancock should have been able to fight all day against anything that could have been brought against him, in such an enterprise, provided the V and VI Corps did their duty, as they were sure to do, at the old Wilderness Tavern.(137)

The II Corps lead division, however, made a 180-degree turn in accordance with Meade's orders. Hancock had received the 10:30 order at 11:40 A.M. Birney on Brock Road, now became the lead division, followed by Mott and Gibbon, with Barlow still bringing up the rear.

Getty's division barely won the race to the Plank-Brock crossing as the federal cavalry, which had been holding up A. P. Hill's Confederates at Parker's Store, went high-tailing it by in the opposite direction just about noon. The communications between Grant, Meade and Hancock continued to be bad. Meade sent two communications to Hancock, at 12:00 and 1:30, saying he was needed to attack up Plank Road with Getty and emphasizing the difficulties the V Corps was having. Neither of these communications reached Hancock until after 2:30 P.M. To further confuse the situation, Hancock and his staff had ridden ahead to the Plank-Brock crossing and their presence had been misinterpreted by Meade as his main force.

Edward Steere, in his study of the Wilderness, writes:

[It] seems incredible that a tactician of Meade's ability—one described by Lee on the eve of Gettysburg as a general who would make few mistakes—should have construed the reported presence of Hancock's headquarters party as equivalent to a heavy attack column standing in readiness to attack. Yet just such a miscalculation was made. The extent of Grant's participation in this blunder cannot be determined.(138)

Steere points out that Meade knew exactly where Hancock's divisions were when they were put into reverse, and it should have been relatively easy to estimate how long it would take them to get to the Brock-Orange Plank road crossing and be ready for combat. "While the leading division would reach the Crossing about one hour after commencement of the movement, it would be unreasonable to expect that Barlow's rear division, the strongest numerically in the corps, could close up and form in battle order much before 6 o'clock."(139)

Walker elaborates on the problems of the march:

It is no small matter to bring up twenty-five to thirty thousand men by a single road and form them for battle; and the difficulty was, in the present case, increased by the narrowness of Brock Road, and the density of the woods on either side. The greatest efforts of the staff were put forth to hasten the work; to get the artillery out of the way and to push the infantry forward.(140)

A huge cloud of dust heralded the arrival of Birney's Division just after 2 P.M. Mott's Division reached the crossing and generated a similar cloud an hour later. Somewhere in that cloud of dust was Private Blood.

For the next hour, the 11th Massachusetts hurriedly threw up breastworks on Brock Road. About 5 P.M. it formed into battle formations, and plunged into the thicket. Captain Munroe's Company K morning report shows that on May 5th there were two officers and thirty-seven enlisted men present, and twenty-two muskets. Late that day six privates of Company K were wounded, including Samuel Blood, whose military service record indicates that he was wounded in the right arm by a minié ball and that his arm was amputated at the shoulder at the II Corps field hospital the next day.(141)

Private Blood had passed the "show blood" test invoked that day by Colonel Blaisdell and described by Captain Blake.

The wounded and dying were borne upon stretchers to the hospitals in the rear; and the usual number of skulkers sought to escape the perils of the battle by traveling in the same direction, and eluding by ingenious devices and shams the vigilance of the provost guard. The colonel halted this class of persons whenever they passed through the regiment and detained them if he was satisfied that they were neglecting their duties. Many conversations like the following ensued between the colonel and the members of these squads; and the questions and answers show clearly the rank and intentions of the parties, without any explanation:

"My good man, where are you going?"

"I'm sick, and the captain told me to go to the hospital."

"You are very weak, and find it hard to travel?"

"Yes; I can hardly walk."

"The hospital is two miles from here; and you are used up, and can't go there. Rest here with my brave men; and I will take your name, and notify your officers if you are killed or wounded."

The soldier, knowing he could not extricate himself from the toils of his pretext, usually pleaded another, which was equally shallow; and sometimes attempted to run away. The colonel at once denounced him in language which could not be strengthened in its style, and concluded by uttering his customary orders upon similar occasions.

"Captain—, detail one of your trusty men to report to me with a loaded musket."

"Private—, you are responsible for this cowardly skulker. If he tries to get away, blow his brains out; but if we are fighting crack his skull with the butt of your gun, and he will never trouble you again."(142)

Of all battles of the Civil War, what went on at the points of collision of the two armies in the Wilderness seems the most mysterious, particularly on the first day, May 5. The action was difficult to observe because of the terrain, and confusing in the reports. Lieutenant Schaff related one incident at Brandy Station in the preceding winter relevant to the problems of reporting of military engagements:

[John B.] Batchelder, whose map of the battlefield of Gettysburg is authority, and whom we had fallen in with while we were there, asked to join our mess at Brandy when he came to the army to verify the positions of the various commands. One night, just after we had sat down to dinner, he entered quite tired. "Well," he announced, taking his place at the table, "I have been in the II Corps today, and I believe I have discovered how Joshua made the sun stand still. I first went to —— regiment and had the officers mark on the map the hour of their brigade's position at a certain point. Then I went to —— regiment in the same brigade; they declared positively it was one or two hours earlier than that given by the other. So it went on, no two regiments or brigades agreeing, and if I hinted that some of them must certainly be mistaken, they would set me down by saying, with severe dignity, 'We were there, Batchelder, and we ought to know, I guess,' and I made up my mind that it would take a day of at least twenty hours instead of thirteen at Gettysburg to satisfy these accounts. So, when Joshua's captains got around him after the fight and they began to talk it over, the only way under the heavens that he could ever harmonize their statements was to make the sun stand still and give them all a chance."(143)

This is a wise caveat to remember in the pages that follow. The lack of information and general confusion in the Wilderness was further compounded by the large gaps in time between the battle and the few written reports that were ultimately prepared. For many brigades and regiments there were no reports at all. General Hancock's report for the II Corps was not written until the fall and winter of 1864-1865, long after Meade's deadline. Hancock explained:

The delay in the transmission of this report, its deficiencies in reference to detail of the troops under my command, during the battle, not belonging to the II Corps, and the absence of many details of the movement of brigades and regiments of the II Corps on that field, have been occasioned by the urgent and constant occupation of my time; absorbed as it was by subsequent operations of the campaign, by the total absence of detailed reports from divisions, brigade and regimental commanders, and lastly as has been previously stated, by the nature of the ground on which the battle was fought, which made it impossible to observe the movements of the troops after they had entered the forest, where thickets concealed the various incidents of the fight from all those who were immediately engaged.(144)

The experience of the 11th Massachusetts and the Second Brigade is a good example of the problem. By report time, the veterans of the 11th Massachusetts had been mustered out, the regiment was a battalion, and its commanding officer, Colonel Blaisdell, had been killed. Colonel Brewster never wrote a brigade report because he apparently became ill and retired the first day of the Wilderness. In the preceding campaigns there had usually been intervals between the significant battles when the commanders had a chance to catch up with their paper work. Beginning at the Wilderness, and up until August 1864, virtually no reports were written because of the constant fighting and tactical maneuvers. Walker writes of the May-July period:

Men, more than there were remaining in the original regiments, were, on a single day, to be poured into the corps, and the new body, thus composed, was to be thrown into one of the most furious campaigns of human history, the strength of a regiment, the strength of a brigade, to be shot down in a day, with as many more the next; a month to be one continuous battle, only interrupted by long and fatiguing marches; two, or three, or four officers commanding the same regiment or brigade in a single week. This, with no long, benign intervals for rest, for healing, for discipline, for mutual acquaintance, was to be the experience of the II Corps, in the months immediately following. . . .(145)

Captain Blake's description of the first day, long on the treatment of skulkers, is admittedly weak on the big or small picture of the battle. He wrote:

This chapter, it may be needless to remark, does not narrate the move-ments of the entire army, because the character of the country, and position of the author with the rank and file, limited his view; and the incidents of a part of the lines, that extended five miles, are described. The division hastened to the vital point, which it reached in the afternoon, and remained in the reserve, rushing from post to post, until 4:10 P.M., when the musketry in front assumed the prolonged roll that always marks a heavy engagement. . . . Breastworks were hurriedly constructed to defend the Germanna Ford Road [it was really Brock Road] and the dry logs of which they were principally composed were easily set on fire, so

94

that it was often necessary to remove a part to save the rest. Sunset came: the darkness of the night followed, but did not check the din of the conflict, which continued when the combatants were unable to perceive friends or enemies, and suddenly ceased at eight, P.M. The Union forces did not yield a single position; and every attempt which was made by Lee to overpower the columns that were advancing by the flank was successfully baffled.(146)

There is fragile evidence of the Federal attack in late afternoon of May 5, but one of the problems that developed from poor communications with headquarters was how Hancock would carry it out. Hancock had answered the delayed communications from Meade at 2:40 P.M.:

Your dispatches of 12 P.M. and 1:30 P.M. received. I am forming my corps on Getty's left, and will order an advance as soon as prepared. The ground over which I must pass is very bad—a perfect thicket. I shall [form] two divisions with brigade front. General Getty says he has not heard of Warren's left, probably because he has not advanced far enough.(147)

Steere writes that Hancock's dispatch "clearly indicates that Getty and Birney were to attack in column of brigades. Getty on the right, Birney on the left, with Mott in reserve. That is, the two assault divisions were to advance on a two-brigade front, both divisional elements having uniform columns of three brigades in depth. Mott's two-brigade division would stand in reserve."(148)

One seeming flaw in this analysis is that Birney's Division, like Mott's, had only two brigades. This became somewhat academic, however, because Meade sent Lieutenant Colonel Lyman to Hancock at 3:15 P.M. with orders to attack "at once." Lyman reached Hancock at 4:05. Meade also specified the attack formation: one II Corps division on Getty's right and another on his left and the other two divisions in reserve "or such other dispositions as you may think proper."(149)

According to Steere, the mechanics of setting up this alignment were not easy.

Hancock was confronted with the problem of executing a difficult maneuver on short notice. Although two of his divisions were still in march column, he considered that Meade's order left him no discretion but that he must attack with the two divisions in hand. He instructed Birney to move by the right from his position between Getty and Mott, and then connect on the right of Getty's moving line of battle. Mott in turn received instructions to leave his trenches and rush through the woods at a right oblique until he joined Getty's left. With Getty in motion toward the enemy, the maneuver was a dangerous one. A double shift by the two II Corps divisions not only uncovered Getty's left at the jump off but involved the risk of bringing up the supporting formations on both flanks in broken lines, thus diminishing the impetus they might otherwise have lent the final shock, or so reducing the firepower, in the event of an enemy counterattack, as to become ineffective or even harmful.(150)

Getty's attack, launched from his right about 4:15 P.M., became hotly contested after about a half mile into the thicket. After a time, Getty was able with great difficulty to establish a connected line but his left flank was precarious. The fighting had been severe, and Getty was convinced he was facing A. P. Hill's full III Corps, rather than just Henry Heth's Division. He called on General Birney for aid and Birney sent Alexander Hays' brigade down Brock Road in an attempt to form on the right of Getty's division. Birney's other brigade, under General J. H. Hobart Ward, was placed in reserve behind Getty's line. Three of Ward's regiments were sent forward to reinforce Getty, with particular attention to his threatened left.

A little after 5 P.M., Mott's Division was ordered to attack. McAllister's First Brigade was on the right and was supposed to form a line with the left of Getty's line. The Second (Excelsior) Brigade was on the left of McAllister and was apparently under the command of Blaisdell who had replaced Colonel Brewster, although Blake locates him with the 11th Massachusetts.(151)

The difficulties of aligning the forces in the thicket became a reality. McAllister's regiment on the right came in behind Getty's left regiment while Mott's division was generally in a right oblique to fill in for the Birney brigades that had been moved to bolster Getty. The crowding from the right and left was felt in the center of McAllister's line which could not form in two ranks as they had on the Brock Road. The commander of the 7th New Jersey, Captain Thomas C. Thompson, stated that forming a line was "almost impossible, as nearly the whole regiment had become overlapped by other regiments on right and left."(152)

About this time the left of Mott's Division encountered the right of General Henry Heth's Division, the brigade of Virginians under Henry H. Walker, who were entrenched on a small ridge in the thicket. They poured out a devastating fire. The 1st Massachusetts was on the left end of the McAllister Brigade's first line and Cudworth, its historian, reported that

The men went forward, however, in very irregular lines, and keeping as closely together as they were able. They had advanced thus only 500 or 600 yards from the road when, directly in front, the unseen enemy opened a double volley, which sent thousands of bullets crashing through the woods into their faces. This fire, so sudden, so unexpected, and so deadly, was returned in but a feeble and scattering manner, because the men were so generally separated from their officers and so apart from each other, besides being perplexed in forcing their way through the tangled forest, that they were comparatively without organization. The enemy answered with another terrific volley, which told with deadly effect upon the foremost groups struggling along to get into some sort of fighting array, killing and wounding a large number and straightaway forcing the rest to fall back. Along the whole division the movement became at once and rapidly retrograde.(153)

Colonel McAllister blamed the Excelsior Brigade for the initial collapse of the line on the left, that was followed by the 1st Massachusetts and the rest of his brigade. He reported that "To assign a cause for this panic is impossible, unless it was from the fact that a large number of troops were about to leave the service."(154) Steere, on the other hand, notes the report of the commander of the 73rd New York of the Second Brigade, which states that the Excelsior had successfully formed in two lines. Lieutenant Colonel Michael Burns reported that the second line had come to the rescue of the first line.

The works were scarcely constructed when the first line of battle was fiercely assailed by the enemy. After a stubborn resistance it was forced back and the second line was ordered forward over its works to its support. The advance was accordingly made, and this command advanced into the woods to the distance of, perhaps, one-quarter of a mile. The first line having broken and fell back this command was soon attacked, and after sustaining the shock for fifteen or twenty minutes, when it was discovered that the enemy had thrown a heavy column on our left flank, and the [Excelsior] brigade was obliged to fall back to the breastworks which had been thrown up by the first line, which was done in good order. The enemy followed up his temporary success, but on coming within range of the breastworks they were most signally repulsed.(155)

The casualty statistics for the Second Brigade, which are very uneven by regiment, tend to support Burns's report that the second line stood and fought for a considerable time. About three fourths of the Second Brigade's killed, wounded and missing (KWM) in the Wilderness were in four of the eight regiments: 11th Massachusetts, 75 KWM; 73rd New York, 66 KWM; 120th New York, 61 KWM; 84th Pennsylvania, 48 KWM. One might speculate that these regiments comprised the second line on May 5.(156)

Lieutenant Colonel Lyman was ordered by General Meade to go to Hancock's position and keep him informed of the progress of the II Corps offensive. Lyman wrote in a relatively contemporaneous letter (May 16),

Delightful! At the crossing of the [Brock] with the Plank sat Hancock, on his fine horse—the *preux chevalier* of this campaign—a glorious soldier, indeed! The musketry was crashing in the woods in our front, and stray balls—too many to be pleasant—were coming about. It's all very well for novels, but I don't like such places and go there only when ordered. "Report to General Meade," said Hancock, "that it is very hard to bring up troops in this wood, and that only a part of my corps is up, but I will do as well as I can." Up rides an officer: "Sir, General Getty is hard pressed and nearly out of ammunition!" "Tell him to hold on and General Gibbon will be up to help him." Another officer: "General Mott's division has broken, sir, and is coming back." "Tell him to stop them, sir!!" roared Hancock in a voice of a trumpet. As he spoke, a crowd of troops came from the woods and fell back into the Brock Road. Hancock dashed among them. "Halt here! Halt here! Form behind this rifle-pit. Major Mitchell, go to Gibbon and tell him to come up on the double-quick!" It was a welcome sight to see [Samuel S.] Carroll's brigade coming along that Brock road, he riding at their head as calm as a May morning. "Left face—prime—forward," and the line disappeared in the woods to waken the musketry with double violence, Carroll was brought back wounded.(157)

General Birney had sent the brigade commanded by General Hays to support the right of General Getty's line, and Hays marched down Brock Road past the Plank Road intersection. Just where and how he supported Getty's right or center has been in Steere's words "left as a legacy of the battle of the Wilderness to the military historian for perpetual discussion." He postulates that

> Hays, attempting to execute the plan of forming on the right of Getty's divisional line, went blindly over the low parallel ridges and across intervening swales, with only the roll of musketry through the trees to guide him toward his objective. With battle lines broken, or badly disordered, the units pushed on, all inspired by a determination to march to the aid of men who had attacked in the faith that their II Corps comrades would speedily bring them support. One by one Hays's disjointed elements went into the merciless ambuscade of Davis' Mississippi riflemen [Joseph R. Davis' Brigade, Heth's Division]. Here, in a few frightful minutes, was the bloodiest shambles of the Wilderness. The blinding flash of a volley, fired at forty yards range, proclaimed the presence of a lurking foe. A counter volley, in which many of the roaring rifles fell from the hands of desperately wounded men, told the Mississippians that they were being attacked by numerous foe, determined to stand and shoot it out. While Davis' men enjoyed the initial advantage of surprise, this was offset by the splendid discipline of Hays' regiments; surviving the first blast of Davis' fire, Hays returned to the thundering fray with a decided preponderance of rifles. As the answering roar of confederate volleys diminished in intensity, the federal brigadier attempted to straighten his lines. Indifferent to the hail of minié balls tearing through the foliage of the trees, Alexander Hays went about the work as coolly as though forming his brigade for a general review. While riding along the half completed line, a whizzing projectile struck his forehead and entered the brain.(158)

General Hays is Mourned

The general who had to listen to Henry Blake's endless exceptions and objections at the Brandy Station courts martial just a month ago was dead. His body was borne to the rear by his grieving staff. Years later, Francis Walker gave an eulogy for the fallen Hays and a rebuke to the leadership that brought him to this forsaken locale.

Among the killed of that afternoon was General Alexander Hays. At Gettysburg, at Bristoe, at Mine Run, at Morton's Ford, this devoted officer rode, with his staff and flag behind him, the mark of a thousand riflemen, the admiration of two armies, only to fall in a tangled wilderness where scarcely a regiment could note his person and derive inspiration from his courage and martial enthusiasm. The contrast had a significance extending far beyond the single loss of a brave commander. All the peculiar advantages of the Army of the Potomac were sacrificed in the jungle-fighting into which they were thus called to engage. Of what use here were the tactical skill and the perfection of form, acquired through long and patient exercise; of what use were the example and the personal influence of a Hays or a Hancock, a [John R.] Brooke or a Barlow? How can a battle be fitly ordered in such a tangle of wood and brush, where troops can neither be sent straight to their destination nor seen and watched over, when, after repeatedly losing direction and becoming broken into fragments in their advance through thickets and jungles, they at last make their way up to the line of battle, perhaps at the point they were designed to reinforce, perhaps not . . . so that the extremity of valor shall be useless; so that the highest soldiership shall be in vain; so that brigades shall not know whether the fire from which men are dropping by hundreds in their ranks comes from the foe or from their own comrades who have lost their way in the tangled forest. It will never cease to be an object of amazement to me that, with such a tract in prospect, the character of it being known, in general, to army headquarters through the Chancellorsville campaign, in which General Meade and General Humphreys had taken a prominent part the year before, a supreme effort was not made, on the 4th of May, to carry the Army of the Potomac either through these jungles toward Mine Run, or past it, toward Spotsylvania. . . . As it was, of the one hundred and fifty guns accompanying the infantry corps into the Wilderness, there was not real use for one third in that battle; while the ablest general was able to control his men and influence their action in only the faintest and remotest degree.(159)

The admiration for General Hays was widespread. Grant, who had known Hays at West Point and in the Mexican War, wrote: "With him it was 'Come, Boys,' not 'Go.'"(160)

Henry Blake, who might have had reason to be unhappy with the presiding officer at the Brandy Station court martial, wrote that Hays was "one of the most fearless and honorable officers in the national forces, whose preeminent gallantry infused confidence upon doubtful fields."(161)

Lieutenant Colonel Lyman wrote of Hays:

He was a strong-built, rough sort of man, with red hair, and a tawny, full beard; a braver man never went into action, and the wonder only is that he was not killed before, as he always rode at the very head of his men, shouting to them and waving his sword.(162)

One dissenting voice on General Hays comes from an unexpected source. Henry L. Abbott, then the captain of the 20th Massachusetts, describing the fight of the II Corps on Cemetery Ridge at Gettysburg the year before, wrote to his father:

The rows of dead after battle I found to be within 15 and 20 feet apart, as near hand to hand fighting as I ever care to see. The rebels behaved with as much pluck as any men in the world could; they stood there against the fence, until they were nearly all shot down. The rebels' batteries, seeing how things were going, pitched shell into us all the time, with great disregard of their own friends who were disagreeably near us. Gen. [Alexander S.] Webb, who commands the Philadelphia Brigade, in his official report has given [Norman J.] Hall's brigade the credit for saving the day, after his own men had run away. A miserable rowdy [Brig. Gen. Alexander] Hays, commanding the 3rd Division, of our Corps, who was not all in the musketry fire, claims I believe, all the credit of the thing. So look out for false stories in the papers. Don't confound this fellow with [Brig. Gen. William] Hays, who is said to be good officer and got up just after the fight.(163)

There was a bit of the rowdy in General Hays if the account of the historian of the 14th Connecticut was correct in describing the action of the Third Division at Morton's Ford about three months earlier. Charles D. Page reported that during the chilly Rapidan crossing in February 1864,

Alfred Waud drawing, Library of Congress
A late evening reconnaisance at Morton's Ford. General Hays got thirteen holes in his clothing, "but not a scratch on [his] body," he reported.

> General Hays rode back and forth upon his galloping steed, his reckless manner and incoherent language indicating that he had added two or three extra fingers to his morning dram.(164)

There was also an account of a remarkable early evening encounter of a group of 14th Connecticut soldiers and their division commander. They were on the right of the Union skirmish line at the Morton House and were firing on the enemy from some of the outbuildings:

> Presently an officer dashed up to the house, dismounted, entered and with various expletives, better imagined than written, wanted to know what they were doing there. It proved to be General Hays who, unaccompanied by any of his staff, had come out to the skirmish line.

Hays ordered the soldiers out of the house and forward. The Confederates had heard the expletives, and when Hays left the house he was shot as he mounted his horse. They ordered the Union soldiers to surrender, stating, "As to your general, we have killed him." Fortunately, the Confederates had only hit Hays in his saddle, and he was able to remount and slide away into the darkness. The soldiers, however, had to surrender and were off to Libby Prison.(165)

Very appropriately, Hays died with the regiment he had raised and referred to repeatedly in his letters—the 63rd Pennsylvania Volunteers. His last letter to his wife, containing a quotation from Byron's "Siege of Corinth," shows his sense of humor as well as a premonition of his death.

The sun and I arose at the same time this morning, and "Joe" sounded his bugle to announce that we were both up.

Yesterday evening we were afforded a most splendid spectacle of a tornado. All the dust of all the army got on a rampage, and for a time overwhelmed us. We watched it approach for an hour, and then it almost overwhelmed us. Tents went up like paper kites, and some scenes were almost ludicrously amusing.

My stable was blown to bits, and in the midst of the storm I was forced to go out to calm Secessia. Solomon was furious, the mule and the cows stampeded, and we had a great time.

This morning was beautiful,

"For lightly and brightly shown the sun,
As if the morn was a jocund one."

Although we were anticipating to move at 8 o'clock, it might have been an appropriate harbinger of the day of regeneration of mankind, but it is only brought to remembrance through the throats of many bugles the duty enjoined upon each one, perhaps before the setting sun, to lay down a life for his country.(166)

Secessia and Solomon were the general's horses. The Garibaldi Guards had reservations about "serving under old Hays," but the general's horses may have had an even stronger case. On March 22nd Hays wrote to his father:

I have had so many shots in my horses since the war began that I am unable to enumerate them. Dan, after having received five balls in previous actions, lost a portion of one hoof by a shell, and fifteen minutes afterward was killed by a cannon-ball through his heart. This was at Gettysburg. Leet had received two balls in previous engagements and at Gettysburg was completely riddled. I did not attempt to count his wounds; perhaps I could not have done so, for he was covered with blood. He died in Gettysburg. In our last action at Morton's Ford Solomon was shot twice, one ball passing entirely through his body; one ball lodged in the saddle; my clothes were cut thirteen times; three holes in my drawers, and yet not a scratch on my body. Is it not Providence? . . . You will think this is a horse letter perhaps, but when you were forty-four you loved horses. I have one more still to introduce—my mare Secessia. She has been in the thickest fight, but has never been touched. She is as beautiful, brave, swift and docile as ever an Arab owned.(167)

Captain James Hamilton

Captain James Hamilton of the court martial board, a company commander of the 105th Pennsylvania in Hays' brigade, also died in the Wilderness. The surgeon for the 105th wrote to his wife on May 7:

We have experienced one of the hardest fights of the last two days we have ever had. Our troops have behaved splendidly—especially our Division. Our Brigade is all cut to pieces. Lost our Brigade Commander Genl. Hays, and 1700 men. Col. [C.A.] Craig and Lt. Col. [Jacob R.] Greenawalt are both seriously wounded. The latter, I fear will die. Capt. Hamilton and Capt. [William J.] Clyde were both killed. In fact, the Regt. is all used up. The fight is not decided yet. Still we all feel sanguine of victory.(168)

Renewed Offensive

With the infusion of the brigades of Samuel S. Carroll, Webb and Joshua T. Owen from Gibbon's Division, the Union forces resumed the offensive on May 5, pressuring the Confederate forces on Plank Road. Lee ordered Cadmus M. Wilcox's division to support Gen. Heth. The brigades of generals Samuel McGowan and Albert Scales were initially successful on Plank Road. They broke through Carroll's line and captured the federal artillery that had been raking the road. But Carroll counter-attacked and forced McGowan back.

back. Scales on the south side of the road, at first successful, was now also forced back.

Barlow's Division, the last division on the II Corps' march, was ordered late in the day to attack the Confederate right flank. Hill rushed up the last two brigades of Wilcox's Division to protect it. General James Lane's Brigade of Wilcox's Division was sent to the right to meet Barlow's flanking action and, as the last daylight was passed, Lane forced John Brooke's Brigade of Barlow's Division back to avoid threatened envelopment of the Confederate lines. Major Peter Nelson, 66th New York, a member of the court martial board, was in Brooke's Brigade.

When exhaustion and darkness intervened:

> The armies did not draw apart. They simply stopped where they were and the regiments and brigades lay all over the Wilderness, facing in every direction, nobody knowing where he or his neighbors or his enemies might be. Northerners and Southerners were all intermingled in the dreadful night, so close together that men were constantly blundering into the wrong camp and being made prisoners.(169)

Chaplain Cudworth of the 1st Massachusetts summarized what happened in the first day in the Wilderness and what all too slowly was being realized by the generals in command as a military fact of life:

> Wherever the Federal troops moved forward, the Rebels appeared to have the advantage. Whenever they advanced, the advantage was transferred to us.(170)

The Second and Longest Day

For those who had survived the first day in the Wilderness, the second was to be equally harrowing and of much longer duration. General Longstreet would introduce a little creativity into the fighting in the thicket. Grant was determined to get at Lee at the crack of dawn, attacking straight up Plank Road before James Longstreet's Confederate I Corps could arrive. Grant wanted to attack at 4:30 A.M. but his corps commanders successfully negotiated a half hour delay. At a little after 5 A.M. General Birney, commanding both his and Mott's divisions, attacked Heth's and Wilcox's divisions of Hill's III Corps and pushed them back. Colonel McAllister successfully right-obliqued his brigade along Birney's left. The Excelsior Brigade was in the second line of the advance. Captain Blake wrote of the renewed offensive:

> The musketry recommenced in the depths of the vast forest at 5:10 A.M. Squads of rebel prisoners were frequently taken to the rear, and many friendly remarks were interchanged; one of them said, "Your fellers went over our breastworks this morning like rabbits." . . . The brigade moved forward at 5:30 A.M., to support the advance, and within a brief period constituted a part of the front, and a fierce engagement followed. The men reclined upon the ground, and returned the fire of the enemy until the forty rounds of cartridges were exhausted. There was a most earnest clamor for cartridges; and the boxes of the slain and wounded were opened and emptied, and a supply of those that were fitted for rifles, but unsuited to the caliber of the smooth-bore musket, was issued to the regiment in this distressing emergency by some blundering officials. The proper balls were brought after a perilous delay, although some of these cartridges consisted of a solid cake of powder; and some exhibited a feeling of discontent because there were no buck-shot. The bullets beat an unpleasant discord by striking the trees, which were clipped from the roots to the top, that was sixty or seventy feet above the ground.(171)

The Union offensive had been quite effective on both sides of the Plank Road. General James Wadsworth's Division from the Union V Corps but now assigned to Hancock, which the previous day had great trouble in negotiating the forest north of Plank Road, came in strongly on the Confederate left. The attack turned out to be a little too strong because Wadsworth crossed Plank Road and got in the way of both Birney and Getty, who were driving up the road. After the Union line was straightened out, the situation of the Confederate III Corps got increasingly desperate. Both the Wilcox and Heth divisions had fallen back and although not routed were in great disarray.

At about 6:30 A.M. Longstreet's I Corps finally arrived ,and General Joseph B. Kershaw, his lead division, passed through the retreating III Corps. Kershaw was able to hold the first echelon of the Union assault force and push them back almost a mile.

Lewis A. Grant's Vermont brigade of Getty's Division in the second line was finally successful in repulsing Kershaw's attack, and Owen's and Carroll's brigades were added to strengthen the Union line.

Charles W. Field's Division of the I Corps was assigned to the Confederate left on Plank Road and John Gregg's Brigade (Texas) and Henry L. Benning's Brigade (Georgia) attacked Birney's brigades and then fell back to their lines. E. McIver Law's Brigade (Alabama), commanded by Colonel W. F. Perry, faced Wadsworth, who initially attacked strongly but then was subjected to a severe counter attack. Wadsworth's division was routed between 7:30 and 8:40 A.M. of this long day. Webb's Brigade was moved forward and ran into Perry's advancing forces who were following Wadsworth. After heavy fighting Webb was able to stabilize the line. A pause in the fighting ensued, which allowed Wadsworth time to reform his division.

About 9 A.M., after the short lull, a Union force consisting of the brigades of Birney, Thomas G. Stevenson (a division from General Ambrose Burnside's IX Corps assigned to Hancock), Mott and Wadsworth, and the brigades of Webb, Carroll and Owen from Gibbon, once more launched an attack up Plank Road.

The Confederates not only held off the renewed offensive, but while this was going on Longstreet was able to organize an expedition to go around the Union's left flank. Four Confederate brigades were marched along the bed of an unfinished railroad track, which formed the hypotenuse of a triangle with the Plank and Brock roads as the other sides. The troops in the railroad cut could not be seen by the Union troops, and they emerged on the left flank of Mott's Division.

There already had been confusion on the Union left. Gibbon had been ordered about 7:00 A.M. to launch an attack with Barlow's Division on Longstreet's flank. Steere states that "the caution that prompted General Gibbon in giving only a tardy and incomplete compliance with Hancock's direction invited the disaster that usually attends a policy of timidity."(172)

Colonel McAllister wrote of the rather strange happenings:

I was informed that my left would be protected by General Barlow. I saw no connection. At one time I saw a line drawn up facing to my left, and felt that all was right; in a short time it disappeared. Feeling some apprehension for my left I reconnoitered and saw nothing.

In a short time, Colonel [Paul] Frank, of General Barlow's Division, came with a few troops, and said that he wished to pass through my line to the front. I told him that I had skirmishers out, that I was advancing with the line of battle and did not wish him to go ahead of me, and that I understood that he was to protect my left, that I had orders to advance when his line advanced, and halt when it halted. He replied that he had orders "to find the enemy wherever he could find him, and whip him." Saying this, he spurred his horse, faced his men to the left, and soon engaged the enemy. But a very little firing took place until some of his men came back running and a verbal message came for me to relieve him. This I declined to do, as my orders were to advance with his line. A few minutes more and all his troops came running back. I had my men stop them [at this time McAllister commanded only three regiments: the 8th New Jersey, the 16th Massachusetts and the 26th Pennsylvania], and refused to let them through. Colonel Frank said to me, "I want to get ammunition." I asked him where. He replied, "Away back in the rear." I informed him that mules loaded with ammunition had just come up on my right and if he would detail a few men I would send them a sergeant and get the ammunition, which could be in a few minutes. At this time the pickets became engaged and I opened my ranks and let Colonel Frank's command through, as I supposed, to get ammunition. This is the last I saw of him or his command. This was near 9 A.M.(173)

This appears to have been Gibbon's tardy and ineffective response which Steere describes as "Frank . . . stumbling through the woods somewhere on Birney's left."(174)

Another of the Wilderness mysteries is Frank's Brigade. They must have found a lot of Confederates for they suffered the greatest number of killed, wounded, missing and captured than any brigade in Barlow's division: 482 in the aggregate. These must have been incurred primarily on the second day, for the other three Barlow brigades were used in the early evening offensive on A. P. Hill's flank on the first day. An April 15th letter from General Hays presents an interesting aside on Frank's Brigade:

I have another episode (as Artemus Ward would call it) to relate. My old Harper's Ferry brigade had prepared an enthusiastic reception for me on the occasion of a trip through their camp, but the Dutch colonel [Frank] who now commands the brigade, hearing of it, forbade. I do not admire such military exhibition, but it indicates the influence I exercise over the troops, and as such is flattering. I am informed that the frequently expressed sentiment is uttered aloud in the brigade, "We fights mit Hays; we runs mit Frank." But I am sure they will never run. God bless them for their devotion!(175)

General Hancock wrote in his report, "I do not know why my order to attack with Barlow's division was not more fully carried out, . . . but had my left advanced as directed by me in several orders, I believe the overthrow of the enemy would have been assured."(176)

At the time of Longstreet's flanking action, a couple of hours later, the fighting had almost stopped and it was particularly quiet on the left. Colonel McAllister in his report declares that he was suspicious that something was going on and made a personal reconnaissance. He discovered the presence of Confederates, but, while he was searching for General Mott with the news, the four Confederate brigades attacked.(177) Steere writes that "McAllister appears to have made no disposition to meet an attack on his flank."(178) In his report, McAllister indicates he was relying on Barlow's Division, although the encounter with Frank was such that would not generate much confidence.

The general failure to detect Confederate movement is hard to understand since such movements on the left, most of which turned out to be of a phantom nature, were almost an obsession with Union headquarters. Earlier in the morning a provisional force under Gibbon comprising six brigades (Henry Baxter, John R. Brooke, Daniel Leasure, Thomas A. Smyth, Henry L. Eustis and Nelson A. Miles) from a hodge-podge of divisions and corps, was sitting farther down Brock Road, out of action, waiting for Longstreet. Later, a line of convalescents was briefly mistaken for Confederate troops on Brock Road. The effective use of cavalry could have ascertained that Longstreet was not on the Catharpin or Brock roads. It is also remarkable that the Union leaders did not use the unfinished railroad cut as a way to get to Lee's flank. Colonel McAllister described Longstreet's flank attack in his report:

About 11:30 A.M. I heard firing on my left and rear. I soon discovered we were flanked. I immediately ordered a change of front to meet it; ordered Colonel [William J.] Sewell to "change front on the right company, right regiment" which he did. I then ordered "about face, left half wheel by regiments." The line was soon formed, facing the enemy, when General Mott and staff came up and was informed of the difficulty. At this time some troops were engaging the enemy in my front; a few moments more they gave way and I received the fire of the enemy. Held the enemy in front and delivered volley after volley into their ranks, but I soon discovered that they had flanked my left and were receiving fire in my front, on my left flank, and rear. Here my horse was mortally wounded by two or three rifle balls, but still able to move slowly. At this time my line broke in confusion, and I could not rally them short of the breastworks.(179)

Captain Blake writes of the action of the 11th Massachusetts and the Excelsior Brigade, whose location is not established but appears to have been much farther to the right than the McAllister Brigade:

The firing indicated at this time, when the brigade was posted half a mile in front of the [Brock] road, the singular formation of the troops that were invisible upon the right and left. A force which was compelled to leave its position fled through the regiment, when the soldiers supposed that they were retreating to the reserve; and soon a compact mass of men was enclosed in a cul-de-sac, and the foe pressed closely upon the front, rear and left flank. They made a detour to the right, crossed the Plank Road, reached the original line of earthworks at midday; and the ground that had been gained by the corps was lost.(180)

At the other end of the Union line, Wadsworth had been put in command of all troops north of Plank Road. To support Longstreet's flanking move, the Confederates in this sector under Field attacked Wadsworth's troops. Steere writes:

Wadsworth accepted the challenge, striking back with such vigor that the left of the Confederate attack recoiled. The opposing lines stood face to face, gripped in the fury of a blazing fire fight.
    The very intensity with which Wadsworth's troops sustained the action only led to a swift collapse of their lines. Aware that the Federal left was tottering, Wadsworth galloped down the Plank Road to urge a holding attack by Webb's left regiments, which had been extended across the road. Failing to find Webb, who at that moment was engaged on the right of his line, Wadsworth ordered Lieutenant Colonel George N. Macy, commanding the 20th Massachusetts, to charge straight up the Plank Road into the face of the enemy's fire and hold as long as possible. He then sent instruction that Webb ascertain the cause of the disorder on the

left, and gather any four regiments he could find to support the holding attack.

Colonel Macy, according to the report, protested the useless sacrifice that obedience to the General's order would entail. Wadsworth wrathfully replied that if the colonel was reluctant to lead his regiment, he would set the example. Then, waving his sword, he galloped to the front.

Macy promptly ordered the charge; his men swept forward, cheering in defiance of the volley that smote their line. Among the first to fall was the colonel, who was sent to the rear with a shattered foot. The command devolved upon Major Abbott, who was described by both Hancock and Gibbon as one of the most promising officers in the army.

Abbott led the 20th through a storm of musketry up to the enemy's front. As his line reeled under the blast of a volley fired at point blank range, the major fell, shot through the head. In the wild melee that followed, the men of the 20th recovered the prostrate body of their young commander who was still breathing fitfully, and carried him to the rear.(181)

Major Abbott is Mourned

In his first and last battles, Henry Abbott's conduct was remarkably consistent. Hard pressed at Balls Bluff in 1861, he had his company lie prone and return the Confederate fire while he remained on his feet and moved up and down the line, miraculously unscathed.(182) He did the same at the Wilderness, but there he pushed the law of averages too far. Lieutenant Schaff wrote:

[Abbott] then ordered the men to lie down so as to escape a wicked, sputtering fire; but he himself, young and handsome, coolly and without bravado walked back and forth before his line, his eyes and face lit by the finest candle that glows in the hand of Duty. "My God, Schaff," said to me the brave Captain [Gustave] Magnitsky of the Twentieth with moistened eyes, "I was proud of him as back and forth he slowly walked before us." A shot soon struck him and he fell.(183)

Thus ended the life of another member of the ill-starred court martial board. Lieutenant Colonel Lyman, a personal friend, described the scene when Abbott marched by him at the crossing earlier that morning.

Webb's brigade marched along the Brock road, and wheeling into the pike, advanced to the support of Birney. Among them was the 20th Massachusetts. Abbott smiled and waved his sword towards me as he rode by, and I called to him, wishing him good luck; and so he went to his death, as gallant a fellow as fell that day; a man who could right into the fight with a smile on his face.(184)

During a lull in the fighting, Lyman got permission to go to the hospital to see Abbott. He reported:

Two miles back, in an open farm surrounded by woods, they had pitched the hospital tents. I will not trouble you with what I saw, as I passed among the dead and dying. Abbott lay on a stretcher, quietly breathing his last—his eyes were fixed and the ashen color of death was on his face. Nearby lay his Colonel, Macy, shot in the foot. I raised Macy and helped him to the side of Abbott, and we stood there until he died. It was a pitiful spectacle, but a common one that day. I left in haste, after arranging for sending the remains home, for the sudden sound of heavy firing told of some new attack.(185)

19th Maine on the Plank Road

In earlier action, during the fire-fight of the 20th Massachusetts, General Wadsworth lost control of his horse, which dashed toward the enemy line. Wadsworth was shot through the back of the head and fell from his horse mortally wounded. Webb's brigade, in a very tenuous position, was saved by the 19th Maine, whose Company F was led by Captain Isaac Starbird of the court martial board. The Maine regiment, which was returning to the line after replenishing its supply of ammunition, formed along the Plank Road to meet the flanking attack from the left straight on. Colonel Selden Connor, the commanding officer of the 19th, reported that

Wounded Being Removed from the Field

Library of Congress

Ambulance Corps training at Brandy Station.

Library of Congress

In contrast, Alfred Waud's drawing of the removal of the wounded in the Wilderness.

113

In a few minutes the Vermont brigade of the VI Corps (Getty's Division), broke from the woods into the road in a confused mass and streamed down the Plank Road toward the Brock Road. General L. A. Grant, the brigade commander, and other officers were striving to rally them but they were crowded together in such a huddle and the pursuing enemy was so close upon them that it was hardly possible for them to reform. It was on the Plank Road at the left of the regiment and just in front of it. As soon as they were clear of my front, and the enemy was close at hand, I opened fire. I was soon after struck in the thigh by a shot coming from the right and fell by the side of the road. When I was down I saw General Webb just behind me and he asked if I was hit. I was then taken off the field in a blanket by some of my men.(186)

General James C. Rice of Wadsworth's Division succeeded to command and was able to form a line to the left of the 19th Maine, but came under attack both from the Confederates on the left flank and from Field on the right. General Birney finally decided that it would be impossible to form a line on the Orange Plank Road and reported to II Corps headquarters that he "thought it advisable to withdraw the troops from the woods, where it was almost impossible to adjust our lines, and to reform them in the breastworks along the Brock Road on our original line of battle." Steere states that Hancock gave his approval with "a heavy heart."(187)

For the second time in as many days, Hancock's offensive up the Plank Road came to naught. Just as Longstreet's flanking action came to its successful climax, he became the victim of friendly fire. Seriously wounded, he was carried from the field. Longstreet had planned and actually ordered a reverse flanking action. Steere calls it a movement by "inversion" which would have brought his forces around from facing Plank Road to facing Brock Road. Lee, however, with his I Corps commander gone, cancelled the last phase of the Longstreet offensive. He then began to realign his troops for a frontal attack on Brock Road which turned out to be quite time consuming. The wisdom of the decision is still debated. Steere writes:

Within six hours after his arrival on the field [Longstreet] had rescued the Army of Northern Virginia from certain defeat and, turning the tide with swift and brilliant counterstrokes, had prepared the offensive blow that Lee, for reasons that history will not disclose, failed to deal with.(188)

114

During the lull that ensued, the Union troops were able to reorganize. Blake described the situation in the section of the line occupied by the 11th Massachusetts:

The extreme heat of the day increased the fatigue, and tears were shed by some who overrated the serious results of the disaster. The slaughter in many regiments had been large; and at one point the bodies of the killed remained in the places where they fell, and defined with a terrible exactness the position held by Union troops; and a long line of rebel corpses was extended in front of it. Some of the recruits, who joined their commands about forty-eight hours before the army evacuated its winter quarters, were slain in this encounter. One of the flagstaffs of the regiment was severed by a bullet, and each hand of the bearer grasped a piece of it. . . . The dislodgment of the advanced force was not sharply followed by the enemy, and few bullets interrupted the rule of quietness during the succeeding four hours. Squads which had been separated from their companies in the confusion attending the retreat through the bewildering thicket continually reenforced the ranks. The division was posted once more behind the slight breastwork which had been erected upon the [Brock] road.(189)

Steere tells us that "the formation of Hancock's defense is only vaguely known. The II corps divisions were apparently in the line, left to right Barlow-Gibbon-Mott-Birney. Getty took his old position on Birney's right."(190)

The Excelsior Brigade was in the first line on Brock Road. Of the activities of the 11th Massachusetts, Blake reported:

[T]he skirmishers were deployed in its front at 4:00 P.M., and the author commanded the detachment from the regiment. The groups were properly aligned within the next ten minutes, when the tramp of heavy force resounded through the woods. Orders were excitedly repeated, "Forward!" "Guide right!" "Close up those intervals!" and finally a voice shouted, "Now, men, for the love of God and your country, forward!" The legions of Longstreet advanced without skirmishers; the veterans trained by the experience of three years beheld "a horrid front of dreadful length," the muskets of the feeble line were rushed to the main body; and

Edwin Forbes drawing, Library of Congress
Artillery on the Brock Road. There was little artillery in the Wilderness. Capt. Edwin Dow's 6th Maine , Battery F, at the left of the Excelsior Brigade was very effective in raking the attacking Confederates with cannister on May 6.

thousands of glistening gun barrels which were resting upon the works opened, and the fusillade began.(191)

Steere observes:

If the assault had been launched in the hope that a determined rush of bayonets would incite panic among a still disorganized defense, the Confederates had reason to quickly amend the view. As their musketry blazed from a point some distance to the north of the Plank Road and swept down across the front of Getty, Birney and Mott, to the edge of the smoke cloud that hovered over the burning woods, the fire poured back across the barrier was steady, accurate and heavy in volume.(192)

Blake described the action:

The soldiers crouched upon the ground; loaded their pieces with utmost clarity; rose up, fired, and then reloaded behind the shelter; so that the

116

Library of Congress
Civil War artist Alfred Waud shows the Confederates breaching the Brock Road defenses for a brief period on May 6th. Blake likens them to ancient Greek warriors who followed their master's command without scruple.

loss was very slight; while the enemy suffered severely, as the trees were small in size, and there was no protection. The only artillery that was used in the afternoon was planted on the left of the brigade, and consisted of four cannon, which hurled canister, shell and solid shot, until their ammunition was exhausted.(193)

Blake's statement about the artillery indicates that the 11th Massachusetts was at the left of the Excelsior Brigade in the first line.

At this point the battle was virtually a standoff, but Steere notes that the elements now intervened.

The forest fire that had been smoldering in front of Barlow's line slowly spread across Mott's front and now, suddenly fanned by the rising afternoon breeze, swept in rolling billows of smoke across the slashings to Mott's first line of works. The logs caught fire; the defenders backed steadily away, holding alignment in a desperate effort to sustain the defense of their burning rampart. Then through the blinding smoke and flame poured a torrent of flashing bayonets. The fierce, pulse-stirring Rebel yell rang above the thundering tumult. G. T. Anderson's brigade dashed into the breach.

Mott's first line wavered, then gave way in wild disorder. As men of the division that had broken twice in battle during the last 24 hours turned their backs to a third peril, fear spread like the flames that had leapt across the abatis.(194)

Captain Blake's commentary has a somewhat different tone:

Unfortunately, the dry logs of which the breastwork was formed were partially covered with earth; and the flames, ignited by the burning wadding during the conflict—an enemy that could not be resisted as easily as the myrmidons of Longstreet—destroyed them, and every second of time widened the breaches. The undaunted men crowded together until they formed fourteen or sixteen ranks; and those who were in the front discharged the guns which were constantly passed to them by their comrades that were in the rear and could not aim with accuracy or safety. The fire triumphed when it flashed along the entire barrier of wood, reduced it to ashes, and forced the defenders, who had withstood to the last its intolerable heat, to retire to the rifle-pits which were a short distance in the rear. The shattered rebel columns cautiously approached the road; but the impartial flames which had caused the discomfiture of the division became an obstacle they could not surmount. The same misfortune followed the Union forces, and no exertions could check the consuming element; and the second line was burned like the first. The conflagration in the road had nearly ceased at this time; the enemy yelled with exultation; the odious colors were distinctly seen when the smoke slowly disappeared; a general charge was made, which resulted in the capture of the original position; and the pickets were stationed half a mile in the advance at sunset without opposition.(195)

Lieutenant Colonel Michael Burns of the 73rd New York Excelsior, which was also in the first line, reported:

At this time, however, the breastworks, formed as they were of dry logs and brush, caught fire and soon became untenable. The command had also expended all of its ammunition. It accordingly fell back to the second line of works, and afterward was formed as a second line of battle some 300 yards in the rear and resupplied with ammunition. The enemy attempted to occupy the ground so abandoned between the two lines of breastworks, but were received with such withering fire from the troops in the second line that they were forced to retire, leaving their dead and wounded behind them.(196)

McAllister's Brigade held the second line with Ward's Brigade of Birney's Division alongside. McAllister reported:

My instructions to my men were that they must hold this line under any circumstances and at all hazards. Soon the enemy's column charged the front line and the battle raged furiously. Myself and staff rode along my line to prevent our men from breaking if the front line should give way. The first line gave way and we received the shock of battle. My brigade poured volley after volley and held the enemy in check so they could not hold the first line breastworks. The regiment on my right, 16th Massachusetts Volunteers, Lieutenant Colonel Merriam, and 11th New Jersey Volunteers, Lieutenant Colonel Schoonover, on my left, advanced and took possession of the front works. They made handsome charge across the field; everything was now working favorably. In a few minutes my horse was mortally wounded by two rifle-balls. I dismounted and walked toward my line; was hit by a spent ball on or near my old wound that paralyzed my leg, and for the time was unable to perform my duty. Communicating the fact to General Mott, retired from the field.(197)

In a letter to his family on May 7, McAllister wrote:

My brigade was in the second line. The first line fought splendidly until their fifty rounds of cartridges was exhausted. Then our line took the brunt of the battle and done well—yes, fought splendidly and made a terrible slaughter amongst the Rebels. . . . We also had a battle day before yesterday. Our Division did not do well; but yesterday we done so well that we have gained all and more than we lost then.(198)

The traditional view sees a breakthrough of Mott's Division and the line being restored by the charges of the brigades of Carroll and Rice. Schaff writes:

Soon one of Mott's brigades began to waiver and then broke, retiring in disorder toward Chancellorsville. . . . Meanwhile Birney had called on Rice, and Hancock on Carroll; the batteries ceased firing, and together those two fearless commanders with their iron-hearted brigades dashed with bayonets fixed at the enemy and soon hurled them from the works, leaving colors, prisoners and over fifty dead and many wounded within the burning entrenchments.(199)

At 5:25 P.M. Hancock reported the repulse of the Confederate attack to Meade.

Toward the close one brigade of the enemy [Anderson's brigade] took my first line of rifle-pits from a portion of the Excelsior Brigade, but it was finally retaken by Colonel Carroll. The attack and the repulse was of the handsomest kind. Please send me your orders.(200)

Lyman was on the road heading toward Meade when the Confederates got into the Brock Road rifle-pits.

When I got back to the crossroad, I was told the enemy had broken through on the Plank and cut us in two; this turned out an exaggeration. They did get into a small part of a rifle-pit but were immediately driven out leaving nearly sixty dead in the trench at the point.(201)

At 5:05 P.M. Mott's Division in two lines of battle was between Birney and the Irish Brigade of Barlow's Division.(202)

Mott's line had, at worst, only been dented. However, the II Corps supply wagons had been sent some distance toward Chancellorsville, and Hancock's recommendation for not taking the offensive was based in part on the resulting shortage of ammunition. The fighting at the intersection of the Plank and Brock roads had ended.

Where Have All the Privates Gone?

At the end of the second day of battle, Private Blood was at the II Corps field hospital having his arm amputated. With him were five other wounded privates from Company K of the 11th Massachusetts. On the 4th, the day before the battle began, Company K crossed the Rapidan with two officers and forty enlisted men; after two days in the Wilderness, it had two officers and nineteen enlisted men. The number of available privates between May 4th and May 7th dropped from twenty-six to nine, with no desertions or missing in action. The last entry in the Company K day book was made on May 7th. On that day Captain William Munroe was listed sick and the first sergeant was wounded.(203)

The 11th Massachusetts lost sixteen killed or mortally wounded in the Wilderness. It initially reported nine killed, fifty-four wounded and twelve missing. The difference presumably reflects the wounded who subsequently died. This was the greatest number of casualties for any regiment in the Second Brigade.(204) Of the ten companies in the regiment, Company K had the greatest number killed or mortally wounded during the entire war: two officers and twenty-four enlisted men.

Walker points out an interesting statistic on the Wilderness:

A comparison of the proportion of killed and wounded who were commissioned officers, with the like proportion at Gettysburg, becomes highly instructive as the nature of the fighting in the Wilderness. At Gettysburg, of the killed 8.5% and of the wounded 8% were commissioned officers. In the Wilderness but 5.7% of the killed and 5% of the wounded were officers. This great disparity among the killed and wounded was due to the difference in the topographical conditions of the two battles. At Gettysburg the fighting was almost wholly in the open. Here not only had the sharpshooter a chance to do the most mischief; but the higher responsibility of the officers led them, in critical moments, to expose themselves with a freedom which caused heavy additions to the list of casualties. In the Wilderness, the greater part of those who fell were struck by men who could not even see them; sound directed the firing rather than sight. In conditions like those, there was little exposure of officers, and their share in the casualties sank to something very near their numerical proportion.(205)

A related and perhaps significant statistic is that no officer of the 11th Massachusetts was killed or mortally wounded at either the Wilderness or Spotsylvania, although twenty-five enlisted men died in these battles.

On to Spotsylvania

Another fitful night was spent by both forces at close quarters in the Wilderness. Blake notes that the "guards of both armies, in charge of prisoners, frequently lost their way in the labyrinth of stunted oaks, and entered the wrong lines, where the relations of the parties were transposed." He writes that "an enormous quantity of fixed ammunition was expended,—most of the soldiers of the division used sixty or seventy cartridges; and fingers were blistered by the muskets, which became very hot in consequence of the rapid firing."(206)

On the 7th of May, Mott's Division was in the reserve. Blake wrote that an "abstract of my notes shows the slight knowledge that I possessed of the maneuvers of the army and the events that transpired."(207) May 8th saw the 11th Massachusetts back on the picket line, forward of the Brock Road. Grant had decided to slide off to the Confederates' right, which Lee and Richard H. Anderson, Longstreet's successor as commander of the Confederate I Corps, had anticipated. The race for Spotsylvania Court House was on. Warren's V Corps marched down Brock Road toward Todd's Tavern the night of the 7th, while the II Corps was to hold its position and then follow. Blake wrote that at 11:00 A.M. of the 8th, the 11th Massachusetts retired from their picket line to Brock Road. Rations were issued, fires were prohibited, and, Blake noted in the language of those whose terms of service would soon expire, "there was one more day less."(208)

Early the next morning the 11th Massachusetts marched to Todd's Tavern. The II Corps was to prevent any Confederate attempt to come down Catharpin Road and cut off the wagon trains. Captain Blake, showing his normal negative attitude toward Meade, wrote that at Todd's Tavern:

> The column halted near a groups of mounted officers, among whom were Gen. Grant, one of the greatest, and Gen. Meade, one of the smallest, warriors that have led an American army. The corps commanders reported at this hour for instructions; and the attentive soldiers observed, with increased confidence in the successful result of the campaign, that Gen. Meade did not give a single direction and that Gen. Grant alone was the controlling mind. "Gen. Meade is nothing but an adjutant for Gen. Grant;" "I'm of more account with my musket than he is now;" "They don't notice him so much as they do the orderlies," —illustrate the style of remarks that were frequently uttered by the rank and file who

were interested spectators. (209)

Blake also noted that there were insufficient ambulances for the transportation of the wounded and "the generals, with exalted philanthropy, tendered their private wagons, which were used for several days for this object."(210) One may speculate that Private Blood profited from this, although his military records indicate that he did not reach Emory General Hospital in Washington until May 25. There may have been other stops that were not recorded, or he may have been one of the wounded temporarily left behind.

Library of Congress
Alfred Waud drawing of Gen. Mott's Division at the Brown House north of Spotsylvania, May 10-11, 1864.

Blake complained that a sleepless night followed because "an inexperienced heavy-artillery regiment, numbering twenty-eight hundred men, performed picket duty, and continually discharged volleys at the bushes and other imaginary enemies."(211)

Mott's Division was up early on May 10 and moved up Brock Road to about two miles from Spotsylvania Court House. Blake noted that

> the open fields were viewed with delight by those that recalled the horrors of the Wilderness. The skirmishers were deployed, and drove those of the enemy until they reached the entrenchments; and the line of battle was established in an advanced position; and a belt of woods, comprising pines of large growth, intervened between the hostile armies. . . . [T]he cannonading was very heavy during the afternoon; and the floating clouds of dust and smoke upon the left, showed the progress of the corps of Burnside. The division made an unsuccessful charge at half-past five, P.M., previous to which the officers of the regiment were told that there were probably not more than two hundred sharpshooters

behind their works; but the instant that the movement commenced, loud yells arose, which showed the presence of a superior force.(212)

History requires that the "unsuccessful charge" on May 10 needs some elaboration. Mott's attack against a bulging salient in the Confederate lines held by Ewell's Confederate II Corps was supposed to be coordinated with an attack by a brigade and four other regiments from the Union VI Corps, led by Colonel Emory Upton. General Horatio G. Wright, now leading the VI Corps after the death of Sedgwick the preceding day, was in overall charge of the attack. An artillery barrage preceded the attack, and Upton was able to charge out of some woods and surprise the Confederate defenders. His preparations went largely undetected, and he was highly successful in penetrating the Confederate lines, capturing over a thousand prisoners. Without support, however, Upton's troops fell under attack from the flank and at nightfall he was barely able to withdraw.

Mott's Division was supposed to have attacked the very apex of the salient, while Upton was attacking its west side. Originally both forces were to attack at 5:00 P.M.

William D. Matter, a leading commentator on the battle of Spotsylvania, writes "that someone decided to postpone the combined assault from 5:00 to 6:00 P.M., [but whether Mott received the changed order] is questionable."(213)

Matter concludes that Mott "likely" attacked at about 5:00 P.M. This is the time given by Colonel McAllister in his report, that Walker says must "be mistaken in the hour, since it is evident that the attack of Mott was intended to be simultaneous with that of Upton, and must have been set in motion by the same signal, the cessation of our artillery fire in that quarter."(214) Matter adopts the time stated in McAllister's account and concludes that the attack was not at all coordinated. An alternative would be to take Blake's 5:30 P.M. version, which would make the a attack a little more coordinated. Previous notations of time by Blake have indicated that he was quite meticulous in recording such details. A 5:30 P.M. attack time would have contributed more in diverting the Confederate attention from Upton's attack.

General Humphreys' view on the action was that

Mott formed his division for attack in view of the enemy, who made every preparation to meet it. Upton's attack was concealed from their view and was a surprise and the plan of assault, being well arranged and carried out, was a success. The plan and manner of Mott's assault, on the contrary, did not admit of its being a surprise. The formation of his troops probably kept the attention of the enemy upon him, and in that way helped more effectually to conceal Upton's preparations. The failure of Mott's division did more than neutralize the success of Upton. Had Mott joined him, the two pressing forward, taking the enemy on the right and left in flank and rear, and receiving further reinforcements from the VI Corps as they progressed, the probabilities were that we should have gained of Lee's entrenchments.(215)

Walker concludes that "through whatever misunderstandings or misadventure, through whatever faults of officers or men, Mott's Division failed to give to Upton prompt and effective support."(216)
Having said that, he quickly adds:

But the support of Upton should not have been left to a single division. If the position he was ordered to attack was practicable, the assaulting columns should have been backed up by the divisions of the VI Corps, by Gibbon, and by the divisions of the V Corps uselessly engaged in assaulting the centre.(217)

Matter points out that Mott's Division, by far the smallest in the II Corps, was not entirely utilized in the attack.

The number of infantrymen in this attack force is not known. It was probably as low as the twelve hundred to fifteen hundred, as Mott had earlier warned Wright. This would represent four or five regiments at the most. The adjutant of the 15th New Jersey, whose VI Corps regiment along with its sister unit, the 1st New Jersey, would march on the right of McAllister's line, maintained that only two regiments from the II Corps were on their left. Apparently most of Mott's Second Brigade, the old Excelsior, had been assigned to locate Burnside's right.(218)

McAllister in his report notes that his brigade was in the first line with two regiments from the VI Corps on his right, commanded by Colonel Edward L. Campbell. The second brigade of Mott's Division was in the second line.

We moved through the woods and drove the enemy's skirmishers back toward their works. On reaching the open field, the enemy opened his batteries, enfilading our lines and causing our men to fall back in confusion, excepting a small portion of the front line. Colonel Blaisdell, Colonel Campbell and myself consulted as to what was to be done, and concluded that there was nothing left but to fall back, which we did, to the foot of the hill.(219)

The group making the decision to retire further supports the belief that Blaisdell rather than Brewster commanded the Excelsior Brigade at both the Wilderness and Spotsylvania.(220)

In a letter to his wife the day after the attack, McAllister wrote:

The troops whose term of service is just coming to a close do not fight well. I am sorry to say that in our Division we have too many of this kind. In a charge I made yesterday, we were repulsed when we ought to have been successful.(221)

Foote points out that Mott was very successful in diverting attention away from Upton.

As it turned out, he was only too successful, both for this own sake and for Upton's, in carrying out the first half of this assignment. Forming his two brigades in full view of the objective, half a mile away, Mott did such a thorough job of attracting the attention of the rebels (particularly the gunners, who had crowded into that narrow space no fewer than 22 pieces of artillery with which to take him under fire across half a mile of open ground) that his division was knocked to pieces within minutes. Already badly shaken by their Wilderness experience, the troops milled about briefly under this pounding, some of them attempting ineffectively to return fire with their outranged rifles, then scurried backward in confusion, seeking cover and concealment.(222)

Grant put to good use what he learned in the Upton and Mott attacks, and on May 12 Hancock was ordered to attack at the apex of the Salient. The conditions were vastly different, however. The attack was at 4:30 A.M., in rain and fog, and the whole II Corps would participate. Captain Blake reported that

The division re-occupied at midnight the earthworks which it constructed upon the 10th; and preparations were made for a grand charge

126

by the corps, the brigades of which were aligned and assigned to their positions in the course of the next three hours. Nature, that had so often favored the national cause, deployed its powerful forces; the night was darkened by the clouds, which sometimes touched the earth; no camp-fires glowed within the Union lines, while those of the enemy reflected upon the heavens like northern lights. A dense cloud of mist, that concealed every moving body of troops, filled the air at twilight; the column received the final order to advance at 4:40 A.M., of the 12th; and thousands of hearts trembled with anxiety, as they silently and firmly approached the unknown dangers of the rebel stronghold. The pickets, whose vigilance had been lulled by the unfavorable character of the elements, were surprised before they could waken their comrades in the reserve, most of whom were sleeping behind a formidable earthwork, which was gained without firing a shot. While the supports were antici-pating a dreadful volley, a spectacle which seemed like a dream greeted their delighted eyes. The faded banners of ungodly rebellion; two chieftains,—[General Edward] Johnson upon a horse, and [General George H.] Steuart on foot; hundreds of prisoners of different grades; batteries and artillery-horses driven by the happy conquerors,—these trophies of Union success passed to the rear of the scene of action. A shout of joy that burst from the lips of men who were elated by the triumph alarmed the forces which held the second line, that was parallel, with the first that had been taken; and rebels who were subsequently captured stated that army was aroused and saved by this cheering.(223)

Foote points out another major difference between what Mott's Division faced on the 10th and what the full corps faced two days later.

Fearing the worst as they stumbled forward through fog so dense that it held back the dawn, Hancock and his soldiers, were in better luck than they had any way of knowing. For one thing, those twenty-two guns assigned to defend the apex of the Salient up ahead, which they expected to start roaring at any moment, tearing their close-packed ranks with shot and shell within seconds of hearing a picket give the alarm, were no means the threat they had been two days ago, when they all but demol-ished one of these four divisions attempting this same thing on this same ground. They were in fact no threat at all. They were not there. They had been withdrawn the night before, and the result of an overdue error by

Lee, whose intelligence machinery, after a week of smooth if not uncanny functioning, had finally slipped a cog.(224)

The artillery had been pulled back because Lee had gotten the idea from various sources that the Union troops were about ready to withdraw to the Rappahannock, and he wanted the guns in position to move quickly. They had been moved to the base of the Salient and were just returning at the urging of generals Johnson and Steuart when the Union attack broke.

Barlow and Birney were the II Corps divisions in the Union front line, with Mott behind Birney and Gibbon behind Barlow in the second line. The success of the attack became a problem after the initial phase. Walker reported that

As soon as the curve in the clearing allowed Barlow's men to see the red earth at the Salient, they broke into a wild cheer, and taking the double-quick without orders, rushed up against the works. Tearing away the abattis with their hands, [Nelson A.] Miles' and [John R.] Brooke's brigades sprang over the entrenchment, bayoneting the defenders or beating them down with clubbed muskets. Almost at the same instant Birney entered the works on his side, and the Salient was won! Nearly a mile of Confederate line was in our hands. Four thousand prisoners—including Major-General Edward Johnson and Brigadier-General George H. Steuart—upward to thirty colors, and eighteen cannon were the fruits of the victory. Crazed with excitement Birney's and Barlow's men could not be restrained, but followed the flying enemy until their second line of works, half a mile in the rear was reached. There the disorganized masses were brought to a stand by the resolute front presented by the Confederate reserves, true to those traditions which made the men of that army even more dangerous in defeat than in victory.(225)

On the Confederate side, General John B. Gordon was beginning a counter attack and Lee was bringing up additional brigades from the I Corps, now under Richard H. Anderson.

Walker wrote that

On the Union side the confusion had become extreme; the long line formed for the assault had insensibly converged as the Salient was reached, and were heaped one upon another. Carroll's and Owen's brigades, of Gibbon's division which was formed in reserve, had been caught by the wild excitement of the charge, and dashing to the front struggled even past some of the leading troops, and entered the confederate works, on Steuart's lines, almost at the same moment with the brigades of [Nelson A.] Miles and Brooke. McAllister's brigade of Mott's division also pushed forward from the second line, and threw itself over the enemy's works almost simultaneously with Birney's division of the first line. This enthusiasm of the charging column was in itself very commendable; but, taken in connection with the originally dense formation, it had led to an unnecessary and dangerous massing of the troops.(226)

Colonel Burns of the 73rd New York of the Excelsior Brigade, which contained the 11th Massachusetts, reported that

About 6 A.M. of the 12th the regiment was detailed to act as a provost guard to keep back stragglers from the II Corps, which was then charging the enemy's work. In this capacity the regiment advanced through the belt of woods previously mentioned, and on arriving in the open field was ordered to proceed to the assistance of the first line, which was then engaged with the enemy. The regiment then moved rapidly forward over the first line of the enemy (which had already been taken) up to and over the second line, under a heavy fire, capturing 150 prisoners, 2 stands of colors, and 2 pieces of artillery, one of which was turned and used against the enemy with great effect. The command succeeded in getting the prisoners, colors, and guns to the rear, but being entirely unsupported, and the enemy concentrating his whole fire it, the works so gallantly won had to be abandoned, and the regiment fell back to first line of rebel works captured. The loss to the regiment both in officers and men were heavy, especially the former. The regiment remained behind the first line until 2 P.M., when it was relieved again to act as provost guard.(227)

The configuration for the Union line established after the Confederate counter-attack was noted by Walker. "The VI Corps coming up took post on the right of the II, occupying the line from the west angle southward; Mott joined the VI Corps at that angle; Birney came next on the left; then Gibbon; then Barlow."(228)

Blake noted that in the early morning the 11th Massachusetts was temporarily detached to assist the provost guard, but that about 8 A.M.

the author was detailed by Gen. Mott, the faithful commander of the division, to reconnoiter the position of the foe with his company, and report the strength of the force in front, which was invisible on account of a slight elevation that arose between the first and second lines of breastworks. While I was reading at 8:50 A.M. the inscription upon a large flag, from a point of observation that had been gained with ease, my right thigh was affected by the sensation that follows a sudden blow: the muscles of the leg instantly contracted; and I was surprised when I discovered that a bullet had plowed through the flesh.(229)

Long after the war Blake described the incident in more detail.

General Mott . . . knew me and shouted, "Take a dozen men, go up that hill and report what is behind it." There were no pickets in sight, but, when we started, they jumped from the ground and underbrush, and, when we went over the top, they were running down the south side of the hill. Their breastworks protected about 6,000 men; their flags were blowing in the breeze and I was at once conscious of the fact that my small force was between two great armies. The Rebel sharpshooters at once demonstrated in a practical way that we were within range of their rifles. Two of my men were wounded, and I was wounded in the thigh. . . . On my trip to the rear I made oral reports to General Mott and General Hancock, the commander of the Corps, respecting the situation, and delivered myself to the regimental surgeon. "Well, Blake," he said, "you came within a thirty-second of an inch of your life that time." The flesh was torn away from my femoral artery.(230)

Thus ended the war for Henry Blake.

Some of the other participants in the courts martial who were at the Bloody Angle, the west end of the apex of the Salient, or close by it, were not so lucky. Colonel McAllister reported that

In the advance and retreat to this point, regiments, brigades, and divisions, as well as corps, became somewhat mingled together, but to do justice, great credit is due to all. . . . This place now became the assailing point, for the enemy retook the works to our right and determined to dislodge us. Their massed columns advanced again and again, and each time were driven back, but still the battle raged. Heavy masses of our troops held them in check and determined not to let them gain an inch. Irrespective of commands the officer moved forward troops to hold this point. Having now lost the entrenchment to our right, we formed a line in an obtuse angle, but line after line melted away before the enemy's fire and it seemed almost impossible to hold the crest of the hill. The Sixteenth Massachusetts Volunteers was ordered by General Mott from my left to this position. They lost heavily, and brave Lieut. Col. Waldo Merriam, commanding the regiment was killed. Much credit is due to the officers and men of this regiment.(231)

Merriam had earlier in the day already made a major contribution. General Barlow, whose division was to spearhead the attack at the apex of the Salient, was not too happy with the intelligence provided as to the route to be followed. Matter describes the scene:

As he [Barlow] listened to the two other officers voice their displeasure, he began to laugh. Soon he had to grasp his saddle's pommel with both hands to keep from falling off his horse. He jokingly told [Charles H.] Morgan that, when they arrived at their destination, he hoped the troops would be faced in the proper direction, so that they would not march away from the Confederates and have to circle the earth and come up in the enemy's rear.(232)

Barlow, hampered by the rain and fog, sought more information about the terrain. Mott was no help, but as noted by Matter,

Barlow eventually found an officer, Lt. Col. Waldo Merriam, who gave him a small amount of information about the terrain over which the advance would be conducted. Merriam, who was commander of the Sixteenth Massachusetts Regiment, had been Mott's field officer of the day on the eleventh. He had participated in the unsuccessful reconnaissance advance on that day as well as the attacks on the tenth. During these operations, he had glimpsed fleeting views of the area between the Brown house and the Confederate works along the northern face of the Salient. He drew a sketch for Barlow on a wall of one of the rooms in

Library of Congress

Alfred Waud commented on his drawing of the Salient at Spotsylvania, "The bloodiest fighting yet."

the house. From this Merriam explained that a treeless corridor about three to four hundred yards wide extended from below the Brown house south for close to five hundred yards, until it joined the open fields of the Landrum farm. The Federals guessed that, if an advancing column marched down this corridor and kept going straight across the fields, it would eventually strike the Confederate works at the desired point.(233)

Matter also notes Merriam's death and, more generally, the conduct of Mott's Division in the Salient and at the Bloody Angle later in the day

Upton's Brigade retired from the crest at approximately 5:00 P.M. One of the regiments that replaced Upton's men was the First Massachusetts of McAllister's brigade, under the command of Col. Napoleon B. McLaughlen. This unit's term of service had nearly expired and it had been assigned to picket duty in the rear. At 2:00 P.M. Colonel McLaughlen had volunteered to help out up front and had been granted permission to do so. His men moved into Upton's former position on the crest and maintained a heavy volume of fire until long after dark. Lt. Col. Waldo Merriam . . . was killed there along the crest. The troops of Mott's division were regarded by some as the weak link in the chain of the Federal II Corps, but many of them fought very well indeed that day.(234)

Just where the 11th Massachusetts was in line on the apex of the Salient is not clear. Marbaker of the 11th New Jersey states that Mott's Division went in on one line, and it appears that McAllister's Brigade was on the right, next to Wright's Division of the VI Corps. Walker notes that

the division commanders of the corps, and the brigade commanders, with a single exception, won new honors at the bloody Salient. Among regimental commanders, Colonel William Blaisdell of the Eleventh Massachusetts deserved especial mention for unflinching determination in holding his line against the most desperate assaults.(235)

The exception was General Joshua T. Owen, who was placed under arrest by General Gibbon and ultimately court martialed for disobeying orders.

The prosecution's most effective witness at the court martial, Captain Sleeper, was also killed at this time, although the details of his death do not appear in any of the reports. Judge Advocate Bingham was badly wounded in the thigh on May 12th while carrying out his duties on General Hancock's staff.

The fighting went on at the Salient far into the rainy night. Only in the early morning of May 13th did the Confederates slowly and quietly withdraw, unit by unit, to a fortified line a half mile back which had been constructed while the fighting had gone on.

The Hospital System

Although Captain Blake's wounding in the morning of May 12 deprived us of his account of the fighting in the Salient, his note taking continued.

My steps to the rear were necessarily slow; the reserves, the headquarters of the corps, the sentinels of the provost guard, and squads of non-combatants, were passed; and more than two hours elapsed before I arrived at the division hospital, which was two miles from the field. Gen. Hancock was issuing orders to arrest the cowards who were constantly escaping from the front, and exclaimed, "These skulkers wish to enjoy the fruits of victory, but are unwilling to share the dangers to win it."(236)

Blake spoke to the Confederate prisoners who were being cared for.

The rebels frankly admitted that their wounds were better dressed than they would have been if they had not been taken prisoners; and many amicable conversations ensued between those who had been rendered helpless while engaged in the deadly combat. Strange as the statement may appear, the rank and file always expressed the same opinion; earnestly wished to see a united country; indulged in contemplating visions of its strength; and portrayed the resistless power with which the ablest officers, North and South, leading the commands of veterans in a common cause against the English in Canada and the British Provinces, and the French in Mexico, would sweep them in the ocean and gulf. Those who belonged to Steuart's brigade evinced a deep hatred towards him on account of his tyrannical conduct, and hoped he would be treated in the harshest manner by the Union troops. They said, that when the batteries were hurling solid shot against their breastworks upon the 11th, he cooly shouted, "They have thrown balls enough: I hope they will send some chains; and then I can fasten them to the legs of my men, so that they cannot run away."(237)

Major W. G. Mitchell of Hancock's staff included the following in his report on Spotsylvania, which showed that General Steuart was not adding to his friends on the Union side, either.

In the midst of this confusion and crowd a soldier attracted my attention by shouting out to me, "Major Mitchell, here is a rebel general." I at once rode up to General Steuart, who gave me his name and rank, and I directed a captain of the Fifty-third Pennsylvania Volunteers to conduct him to General Hancock. When Steuart was taken to the general, who knew him before the war, held out his hand, saying, "How are you, Steuart?" The latter replied, "Under the circumstances, I decline to take your hand." "And under any other circumstances I should not have offered it," said General Hancock.(238)

As noted previously, Private Blood's arm was amputated on the 6th of May in the II Corps hospital off Plank Road. The medical director of the Army of the Potomac described the II Corps hospital in his report on the Wilderness campaign:

Its hospitals were located near Carpenter's house, 1 mile southeast of the junction of the Germanna Ford and Chancellorsville plank roads. The site a good one, with good water, and two ambulance roads leading to the front, which was only a mile distant. About 600 wounded were received during the day.(239)

Initially the wounded from the Wilderness were to be evacuated back across Elys Ford to Rappahannock Station and then taken by train to Washington. The report of the Army of Potomac Medical Director stated that

All of the army wagons of the general and corps trains which could be emptied were turned over to the medical department during the day (May 7), and by 6 P.M. were being loaded with wounded. These wagons were thickly bedded with evergreen boughs, over which shelter-tents and blankets were spread, and were comparatively comfortable for the class of cases for which they were used. . . . Three hundred and twenty-five wagons and 488 ambulances were used for the wounded of the infantry corps, and it was found absolutely necessary to leave behind 960 wounded on account of lack of transportation (600 of whom were II Corps wounded). . . . On the evening of May 7 it was determined to entirely abandon the line of the Rapidan and the army moved during the night to the vicinity of Spotsylvania Court House. The train containing wounded was, therefore, ordered to accompany the trains of the army to Aldrich's on the Fredericksburg plank road, 2 miles south of Chancellorsville.(240)

On May 9, at 11 A.M., the train of wagons with the wounded reached Fredericksburg.

Captain Blake's exposition of his treatment in the II Corps Hospital at Spotsylvania six days later gives us a pretty good idea of what happened to Private Blood and the others.

MOLLUS-USAMHI

John A. Douglass, surgeon of the 11th
Massachusetts, treated Henry Blake's
wound at Spotsylvania and may have
amputated Samuel Blood's arm in the
Wilderness. Douglass was 33 years old
in 1864.

MOLLUS-USAMHI

Surgeon Douglass, in an undated photo
taken long after the war, probably uniformed to participate in a GAR Memorial
Day celebration in his home town of
Amesbury Mills, Massachusetts.

The arrangement for the treatment of the disabled were most excellent:
a board of experienced surgeons held a consultation upon every case in
which amputation took place; and all that medical skill and attention
could effect was readily performed. The Government supplies were
abundant; nourishment of every description was bestowed; and faithful
nurses often brought the cold water, which was Nature's restoring
liniment, and saturated the bandages. A small strip of white cloth was
fastened to the button-hole of the coat as soon as the names of the
wounded were recorded; and the sufferers of every rank and both armies
received the same kind treatment, and reposed upon beds of pine boughs
in the capacious hospital tents. More than three-fourths of the number
were untroubled by pain; and one man who had lost a leg, "I should think
that my foot was on, for I have a queer feeling in the ankle;" another
replied to this as he raised the stump that had once been the right arm,
"I have the same feeling in my wrist which you have in your ankle."(241)

Library of Congress
Union soldiers wounded at the battle of the Wilderness were taken to Fredericksburg, Va., where this photograph was taken.

Blake after the war noted that it was "Dr. John A. Douglass, surgeon of the Eleventh of blessed memory," who had dressed his wound.(242)

The medical director's report also indicates the very unusual nature of the Wilderness fighting. Of the 2,903 wounded in the II Corps, all but ten were bullet wounds. There were 207 amputations performed on II Corps wounded.(243)

Private Blood's type of amputation is reported in the *Medical and Surgical History of the Civil War*. His is one of the 852 cases of amputation at the shoulder on account of shot fractures. The text states that

a large proportion of these cases were primary operations, practiced on account of shot fractures of the upper part of the humerus, generally with implication of the joint, and with such lesions of the soft parts as precluded a resort to excision. Others were performed on account of consecutive disease involving the upper arm.(244)

An accompanying table shows that 499 of these cases (including Blood) had amputations within 48 hours of the wounding and that 368 recovered, a very favorable rate of 76%. On the other hand, those 157 cases where the amputations were undertaken between the 3rd and 13th day of wounding had a recovery rate of only 54%.

An example of the unfortunate results of delayed treatment and amputation was the Company K's first captain, Benjamin Stone. He lay on the Second Bull Run battlefield for four days before being taken to a hospital and his leg amputated.

Captain Blake described his own transportation from the battle scene as a wounded soldier. He noted that the firing at Spotsylvania stopped on the 13th and that "boughs and leaves were placed in the wagons that were proceeding to Acquia Creek for ammunition, forage and army supplies, to make them suitable for the transportation for the wounded."(245) In the afternoon the long trains of ambulances and the walking wounded headed down Plank Road for Fredericksburg. The devastated and largely deserted city held little solace for the wounded, according to Blake.

The conduct of unscrupulous agents, who acted in behalf of societies that induced the Government to allow them to supply the wants of the disabled at this point, caused a scarcity of food, lack of attendants and universal suffering, to such an extent that many clamored to be sent to the front; and a shout of joy was heard when the matching orders were received. . . . The chaplain who had been dismissed from the service for stealing a horse was very active, and circulated Bibles and tracts for the Christian Commission among the wounded.(246)

The wagons continued their march through the fields of Falmouth where the 11th Massachusetts had camped during the winter of 1862-1863 and reached the Belle Plain Landing on the Potomac on May 15. According to Blake,

the wounds of all were examined before they were allowed to enter the transport, to detect the cowardly imposters, a large squad of whom was sent under guard to the detachment of skulkers, which numbered a thousand. A body of twenty shirking officers, some of whom were in irons, who had escaped from the battle of the Wilderness to Washington, marched by the ambulance; and I could not imagine a stronger cause for the emotion of humiliation and shame which was expressed by their dejected and averted faces. The steamer that had been fitted for its use with commendable foresight before the army crossed the Rapidan was

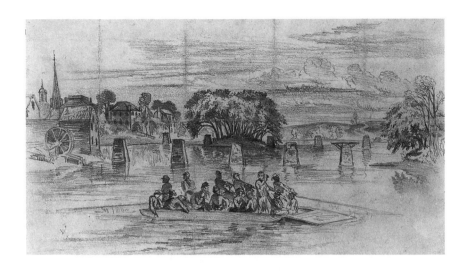

Edwin Forbes drawing, Library of Congress
Wounded soldiers from the Wilderness crossing the Rappahannock at Fredericksburg (May 15) on a flat boat.

amply supplied by the Government with every article that was required for the shattered frames of its passengers.(247)

On the hospital boat Blake "heard a familiar voice in the bunk above and recognized Major Bingham who was also wounded at Spotsylvania Court House."(248)

Blake's praise for the Union medical operations did not extend to the rear echelon medical personnel where the steamer unloaded the wounded.

The strength of the wounded was completely exhausted in Washington by waiting upon pompous and unfeeling officials, who viewed with contempt the men that performed the fighting in the front while they flourished in luxurious ease and safety in the rear.(249)

Blake seems to have reached Washington rather quickly, around the 15th of May. Private Blood's twenty day period before he checked into the Emory General Hospital in Washington suggests the possibility that he was one of the 600 Union wounded left behind in the II Corps hospital. The medical director reported that "hospital tents, medical officers and attendants, medicines, hospital stores and dressings, and three to five days' rations were left with these wounded."(250) The report further noted that "within the following weeks about 1,000 wounded were collected and carried to Fredericksburg by ambulance and wagon trains."(251)

The records show that Blood was transferred to the U.S. Army General Hospital in Readville, Massachusetts, on April 19, 1865. A note from the surgeon indicates it was "for the purpose of being more easily supplied with an artificial arm." On the 25th of April, "for the sake of still, greater facility in this respect," he was transferred to the Soldiers Rest Hospital in Boston. On July 25, 1865, he received a disability discharge with a finding of incapacity because of "amputation of right arm at shoulder joint in consequence of gunshot wound received in action Wilderness, Va., May 5th, 1864, not fit for Invalid corps, totally disabled." Private Blood received a pension until his death in 1925.(252)

The 11th Massachusetts Survives

The reorganization had finished off the III Corps and the Hooker Brigade, and the Wilderness and the Salient at Spotsylvania finished off the Hooker (Mott) Division. According to Walker,

the heavy losses sustained by Mott's Fourth Division during the campaign, together with the expiration of the terms of enlistment of several regiments therein, rendered necessary a discontinuance of that division, its two brigades, one of which General Mott was assigned to command, being attached to the Third Division, General Birney. The Third Division thus came to have four brigades.(253)

The 11th Massachusetts had lost another nine men killed or mortally wounded and thirty-five wounded and four missing at Spotsylvania. Company K, which had numbered only twenty after the Wilderness, showed two more wounded and two missing after the Salient. On the 21st of May some forty-five enlisted men were transferred to the 11th Massachusetts from the 1st Massachusetts whose enlistments had expired. Company K got seven new privates, but lost four more wounded and one missing at North Anna and Totopotomoy Creek before the month ended.(254) In early June, the 11th Massachusetts was lightly engaged at Cold Harbor, losing one killed and nine wounded. The veterans of the 11th Massachusetts were mustered out on June 12, 1864.

The recruits and reenlisted veterans were formed into a battalion of five companies, which was subsequently increased by two companies of the 16th Massachusetts when that regiment was mustered out on July 11. Included among the officers of the 16th so transferred was Richard F. Lombard, one of the defense witnesses and a member of the committee that drafted the protest resolution. This left the 11th Massachusetts as the only remaining regiment from Hooker's Old Brigade. The regiment's historian wrote:

> We had fought together on so many battlefields, that this comradeship of three years service (and such an eventful three years) will never be effaced so long as one is left who won the right to wear the white diamond with "Hooker's Brigade" inscribed thereon.(255)

The 11th Massachusetts fought on for another year and the battles of Petersburg, Strawberry Plains, Deep Bottom, Popular Spring Church, Boydton Plank Road, Hatcher's Run, Weldon Railroad, Farmville and Appomattox Court House followed. On July 14, 1865, the regiment was mustered out on the Boston Commons.

V. Eulogized Heroes and Survivors

Colonel William Blaisdell

Contrary to McAllister's prediction that Blaisdell would leave the service when he lost command of the brigade, he re-enlisted and led the regiment at the battles of North Anna and at Cold Harbor. At Petersburg he was detached from the 11th and put in command of the Corcoran Legion.

> While directing the construction of earth works, he was dismounted, standing upon the raised mound of earth which subsequently became a portion of the main works of the Union army. While thus exposed, he was picked off by a rebel sharpshooter from a window of a house within the enemy lines.(256)

Also contrary to McAllister's prediction that Blaisdell would never get his star, the fallen officer was made a brevet-brigadier general effective the date of his death. It would have pleased him and galled McAllister that he got his star before that of the New Jersey colonel who ultimately ranked him as a brevet-major general.(257) Insight into his life and character, or lack thereof in McAllister's view, remains somewhat of a mystery. The Dorchester *Beacon* of July 22, 1899, printed an article on "The Fighting 11th" which spoke of the first two colonels of the regiment.

> Colonel [George] Clark was never with his regiment after Bull Run. He went immediately to Washington, resigned and went home. It was not lack of courage that caused him to do so, although many of the men believed so. He had a very nervous and excitable disposition and worried continually over his affairs instead of taking things as they came. He

142

almost worried himself into brain fever, and was physically unfit to retain his position. He was succeeded by the lieutenant colonel, William Blaisdell, a man who had served through the Mexican war and who firmly believed that he was not born to be shot.

In his unpublished memoirs Blake wrote that according to Blaisdell, he had served with Grant in the Mexican War.

Grant and Blaisdell were eight years in the same company, 4th U.S. Infantry, Blaisdell being a Sergeant and Grant being a Lieutenant. When the fame of Grant arose above the military horizon in the West, Col. Blaisdell stated often these facts and also, that in the assault on a church in one of the last battles prior to the capture of the City of Mexico, he saved Grant's life. The door was broken open leaving a crevice of two inches and a Mexican was standing inside and raising his gun to shoot Grant when Blaisdell cut him down with his Sergeant's sword.(258)

Blake wrote that Grant was responsible for Blaisdell being given command of the Corcoran Legion, and when he was president having Blaisdell's son placed first on the at-large list for appointments to West Point.(259)

Major Henry L. Abbott

Henry Abbott was one of the most distinguished junior officers of the Army of the Potomac, and according to the author of the history of the 20th Massachusetts,

it is doubtful if there was one of his rank so widely and favorably known in the army. General Meade had become well acquainted with his merits, and intended soon to offer him a position of importance on his staff and a higher rank. The news of his death reached headquarters while the battle was in progress, and General Meade spoke feelingly of it to General Grant while the two were sitting on a log together.(260)

His loss was noted by both General Hancock and his brigade commander, General Webb, who wrote that

his reputation as an officer stood far beyond the usual eulogies pro-
nounced on dead officers. I feel that his merit was so peculiar and his
worth so well known to all the officers of the corps and to the general
commanding, that it is not necessary for me to attempt to do him justice.
My brigade lost in him its best soldier.(261)

After his death he was promoted to brevet brigadier general for his action
in the Wilderness, and at 22 was, perhaps, the youngest of that rank. Until the
Wilderness, he had lived a relatively charmed life. He escaped death or capture
at Balls Bluff, was wounded at Glendale on the Peninsula, fought street by street
in Fredericksburg against an equally brave and stubborn Harvard classmate,
Lieutenant Lane Brandon of the 21st Mississippi(262), and escaped unscathed
in the force that held off Pickett's charge at Gettysburg's Cemetery Ridge. The
fatherly General Sedgwick, who was killed at Spotsylvania three days after
Abbott's death, was particularly fond of the young officer.

Richard H. Dana, the well-known author of *Two Years Before the Mast,*
visited the army during the early days of 1864 and made this entry in his diary
under date of April 26:

Sedgwick spoke in very high term of the Massachusetts regiments,
especially the Twentieth, and of Major Abbott, who now commands it.
He thinks Abbott the bright particular star, though he did not express it
in these words.(263)

The epitaph, "in action he was sublime," was from Oliver Wendell Holmes,
Jr., perhaps Abbott's best friend in the 20th Massachusetts.(264) Holmes'
memories of "Little" Abbott and his experiences in the Civil War, generally,
were very close to the surface during the Supreme Court justice's life. Holmes
wrote of Abbott:

He steered unquestioning not turning back,
Into the darkness and the unknown sea;
He vanished in the starless night, and we
Saw but the shining of his luminous wake.(265)

And in a Memorial Day address at Harvard in 1884, he declared that

144

There is one who on this day is always present on my mind. . . . He was little more than a boy, but the grizzled corps commanders knew and admired him; and for us, who not only admired, but loved, his death seemed to end a portion of our life also.(266)

General Alexander Hays

Forty years after the war, a monument to General Alexander Hays, in the form of an upright cannon, was erected a few yards north of the Plank Road intersection on the Brock Road at the spot where he fell. The unveiling of the monument was on June 5, 1905, on ground donated by former Confederate Major W.S. Embrey, and accepted by veterans of 63rd Pennsylvania. The state's attorney of Spotsylvania County spoke to visitors from Pittsburgh at the ceremony.

Let me assure you that the Confederate soldiers will take this charge, and on Memorial Day they will decorate it with ivy and all the flowers that God gives in the springtime. The Confederate women who honor the memory of the God-like Jackson, will place an equal number of blossoms on the monument to this brave man.

Let me assure you further that when you hear a southern man berating the northern soldier, you hear words of a liar and a cheat. The bitterness after the war came from those who became soldiers only after the war was over and the southerner who would kill all the Yankees now never hurt one in the sixties.(267)

Katherine Tennery
Memorial to Alexander Hays at the Wilderness.

145

A quartet then sang "Tenting on the Old Camp Ground," and a luncheon was served by the Ladies' Spotsylvania Cemetery Association. "Hooray, boys; let's see if the Johnny girls will feed us better than they did forty years ago," shouted one Grand Army of the Republic man, as he dashed for the 1905 meal tent. About one thousand dollars was added to the cemetery fund.(267) The General would have liked his little party. There is also a statue of Hays at Gettysburg, erected by the State of Pennsylvania.

Captain James R. Bigelow

Some of the participants in the courts martial left substantial tracks, but others did not. An examination of the most likely sources has not revealed the fate of the cashiered Captain Bigelow. The roster of surviving veterans (1893) listed in Hutchinson's history of the 11th Massachusetts does include a Captain J. R. Bigelow of Hyde Park, Massachusetts. Apparently the veterans of the 11th Massachusetts did not consider him to be in disgrace.

Lieutenant George Forrest

Following the court martial, Forrest took action to mitigate the verdict of the court. He was successful in getting President Andrew Johnson to remove his disability in late 1865. A letter from General Hancock was primarily responsible for the President's action. Hancock wrote,

> I think it would be well to have the disability in this case removed. I know the circumstance very well and although an example was necessary at the time, yet I was convinced then as now that the origin of the difficulty in which this officer became engaged could be traced to officers higher than those punished.(269)

There is also a letter from General Hooker in the file that supports Forrest's request in 1865 to be appointed an officer of colored troops. Hooker wrote:

Lieut. Forrest is an intelligent and brave officer, and if his services may be taken as a criterion will make a valuable addition to that branch of the Army.(270)

Prosecution Witnesses

Alfred DuPaget's request to leave the Army, which had been turned down before the Wilderness, was finally granted in early 1865. Sergeants Benjamin Morehouse and William Rockhill were eventually mustered as officers in the 11th New Jersey. Morehouse was promoted to captain early in 1865.(271)

Henry N. Blake

B lake arrived back in Boston in early June 1864, a little before the other veterans of the 11th Massachusetts. When the veterans made their last parade through the streets, Captain Blake wrote

I being disabled had the rare privilege of riding in an open carriage and viewing familiar scenes. A grateful people greeted the boys with cheers at every step of the march and an order was published to all to report on the 24th for muster out.(272)

Blake reflected that "I had wasted upwards of three years in mental idleness, and was actually five years behind my classmates remaining at home. And yet, if such a thing were possible, I would not exchange place with any of them."(273)

As he attempted to revive his law practice, Blake wrote his book, which he indicates in his memoirs took a couple of months. In his preface Blake states that during his service "he recorded in the diary every incident of interest which passed under his observation; and the request of many comrades, who saw him take notes upon the march or on the battle-field, induced him to prepare them for general reading."(274)

The country in 1865 might not have been ready for Blake's hard-hitting assaults on some of its respected generals and on institutions as revered as

Christian Commission and army chaplains. His views on the extent of drunkenness among Union officers, and his accounts of individual incidence of such, was probably not much appreciated by the establishment or the public at large.

After the war, Blake took at least one parting shot at General Carr. In August of 1865 he wrote to Secretary of War Stanton requesting some official information as to whether that "notorious coward, scoundrel, perjurer, ignoramus, and Celtic vagabond, Joseph B. Carr of Troy, N.Y.," had ever been confirmed by the Senate.(275) The response to this letter, if any, remains a mystery, but it must have raised a few eye brows.

One might have reasonably predicted that Henry Blake would practice law for the next fifty years in Boston, but post war restlessness seems to have affected him, and in the spring of 1866 he headed for the Montana Territory. Blake blamed it all on an insurance policy examination, from which he learned that he might be susceptible to consumption. As it turned out, his fears were groundless, as he outlived all his law school classmates and a preponderance of the Union army.

[Ed. Note: Blake's post war career is outlined in detail in Appendix B.]

Court Martial Board Survivors

Half of the active members of the board were killed in the Wilderness or Spotsylvania. The remaining four members and the judge advocate survived the war, and three of them were brevetted as brigadier generals.

Colonel William R. Brewster recovered from his illness on the first day of the Wilderness and returned to command the Excelsior Brigade on May 28. He continued in command until it was disbanded in the late summer of 1864 because of the expiration of the enlistments of its veteran regiments. Brewster was mustered out on October 25, 1864, but was made a brevet brigadier general on December 2, 1864. After the war he was an official of the Internal Revenue Service. He died on December 13, 1869, at 41 years of age.(276)

Major Peter Nelson, 66th New York, survived the battles of May and early June 1864, but was captured by the Confederates on June 17 before Petersburg. Barlow's Division had supported the attacks by the IX Corps on the Confederate lines, had captured some strongholds, but was counter-attacked and lost heavily, particularly in prisoners. Nelson was a prisoner of war at Camp Asylum at

Library of Congress

The small footbridge to the right of the high railroad bridge on the Appomattox was the scene of Col. Isaac Starbird's wounding on April 7, 1865.

Columbia, South Carolina, and was paroled in March, 1865. He was discharged on May 5, 1865, and died in 1899.(277)

Captain William McAllister, 140th Pennsylvania, remained a company commander until mustered out on April 11, 1865. He had been wounded at Gettysburg.(277)

Captain Issac W. Starbird was 25 years old when he served on the court martial board and was the commanding officer of Company F of the 19th Maine. Starbird eventually became a colonel and the commanding officer of the 19th Maine. He was made a brevet brigadier general for gallantry in action on April 7, 1865, at the High Bridge over the Appomattox, two days before Lee's surrender. The Confederates had set the railroad and foot bridge on fire in their retreat across the Appomattox. The 19th Maine was rushed forward to put out the fires. Seeing this, the Confederates sent a brigade back to see that the bridges were destroyed. Colonel Starbird was hit while he directed the defense from his horse in the middle of the bridge. Union re-enforcements arrived and the pursuit of Lee continued. Starbird, from Litchfield, Maine, was mustered out on June 7, 1865. He had graduated from Bowdoin College in 1862, and was a merchant after the war. In 1878, he graduated from Dartmouth Medical School and practiced medicine until he died in Boston on February 2, 1907.(279)

Captain Henry H. Bingham was wounded in the thigh at Spotsylvania, and returned to the Army in the late summer of 1864, when he was promoted to major. In November of 1864 General Humphreys replaced General Hancock as commander of the II Corps and Bingham continued on as a staff officer to the new corps commander. It is noted by Walker that two days before the end of the war, at Farmville, the "most gallant and capable staff officer" was again wounded.(280)

Bingham was mustered out of the service in June 1866. By an order of June 22, 1867, he was made a lieutenant colonel by brevet for "highly meritorious services during the recent campaign terminating with the surrender of the insurgent army under General Robert E. Lee." And by an order of October 9 he was made a colonel and then a brigadier general for "conspicuous gallantry and meritorious services during the war." (General Orders 65 and 91, 1867) All were to date from April 9, 1865.

On August 26, 1893, Bingham, then a prominent member of the Appropriations Committee of the U.S. House of Representatives, was awarded a Congressional Medal of Honor "for distinguished gallantry in the battle of the Wilderness, Virginia, May 6, 1864, where he rallied and led into action a portion of troops which had given way under the fierce assaults of the enemy."(281)

[Ed. Note: Bingham's postwar career is outlined in Appendix B.]

Colonel Robert McAllister and the New 11th Massachusetts

Robert McAllister was the commander of First Brigade of Mott's Division through the Wilderness and into the Spotsylvania campaign. Mott's Division was dissolved on May 13th and became two brigades of Birney's Third Division right after the Salient. McAllister returned to command his old regiment, the 11th New Jersey, when General Mott reverted to brigade commander. McAllister was not happy with this situation, and his appraisal of Mott's performance, heretofore quite favorable, became more critical. In late May, 1864, he wrote to his daughter:

Though Genl. Mott is in command of the Brigade, I am always on the front line and in command. They all say that I am the "fighting commander" of the Brigade. The General is in command when all is quiet. His Headquarters are well to the rear, and he don't seem to be anxious to get to the front. However, this is confidential. It seems to be a strange way to do business, but it is.(282)

In late July, General Birney was made the commander of the X Corps and Mott became the Third Division commander. McAllister got his brigade command back, which then included the 11th Massachusetts, inasmuch as the Excelsior Brigade had been disbanded. Somewhat strangely, McAllister appointed Captain Lombard of the 11th Massachusetts, formerly of the 16th Massachusetts, as one of his aides. He must have forgotten Lombard's rather prominent role for the defense in the Brandy Station courts martial, for he states his new aides "are good, brave men, and men of experience, so I will get along. They are all gentlemanly and fine looking aides."(283)

In his letters in the fall of 1864 and the spring of 1865 McAllister writes approvingly of the performance of the 11th Massachusetts on a number of occasions. This regiment was now commanded by defense witness Charles C. Rivers, who had been promoted to major and eventually became the regiment's colonel. McAllister finally got his star as a brevet brigadier general on October 27, 1864, on the basis of his conduct at the battle on the Boydton Plank Road. The 11th Massachusetts played a major role in this battle, and suffered some grievous losses of its veteran officers.

[Ed.Note: The role of McAllister and the 11th Massachusetts in this battle, which had some similarities to the Wilderness, is described in Appendix C.]

McAllister continued as the brigade commander until the end of the war. His name was included in a long list of brigadiers appointed "major general of volunteers by brevet" for "gallant and meritorious service." He was mustered out on June 6, 1865.(284)

[Ed. Note: McAllister's postwar career is outlined in Appendix B.]

General Joseph B. Carr

With the exception of a very brief period as commander of a division of colored soldiers in the front at Petersburg, Joseph Carr spent his last year in the army as a base commander behind the lines. After he lost command of the Hooker Division he reported to General Butler and was placed in command of "the exterior line of defense on the Peninsula, headquarters at York-town."(285)

The Troy *Daily Times,* in a sketch of Carr's career, declared that

At about this time a clique, composed of several unprincipled men and jealous officers, conspired to deprive Gen. Carr of his position by having his nomination rejected by the Senate. Their base charges affecting his conduct and capacity were not sustained, however, and their machinations only resulted in their defeat.(286)

The paper noted that Gen. Humphreys played a major role in the Carr confirmation. Early in July 1864, Carr was ordered to the front at Petersburg and placed in command of the first and third divisions of the XVIII Corps for "the battle which was expected to take place on the following day, immediately after the explosion of the Burnside mine." On October 1st, Carr "assumed charge of the defenses of the James Headquarters at Wilson's landings, a command he held for the rest of the war. In May 1865 he was transferred to command the base at City Point and in June was promoted to Brevet Major-General."(287) In August 1865 he was mustered out.

[Ed. Note: Carr's postwar career is outlined in Appendix B.]

Epilogue

Our examination of life at Brandy Station in the spring of 1864 and the courts martial have disclosed the petty politics and personal animosities that existed in the Hooker Brigade. Although such conditions were not unique in the Army of the Potomac, their presence was highlighted by the explosive reaction to General Meade's reorganization. The reorganization had few defenders, but having successfully passed General Grant, it seemed to gain a life of its own. It attracted little attention in Congress and did not make much of an impression on the public generally. Perhaps they did not understand the significance of a small white diamond patch with the words Hooker Brigade stitched upon it. One can speculate that this indifference was due to the reorganization being perceived as primarily a "technical" matter. The nearness of the spring campaign, and the fear of the disruption a discussion of its merits might have on the war effort may have further inhibited examination of the subject.

Also somewhat surprisingly, the press apparently was not present at the courts martial. The five miles of muddy roads from Culpeper to II Corps headquarters was probably the primary reason, although it may have been considered too controversial to cover. Contrary to General Hays' prediction, the transcripts were not made public and the reorganization, the courts martial, and the reaction of the affected troops was an event generally ignored. The men immediately concerned were left alone, having to bear the burden of being labeled with crimes from insubordination to mutiny.

Additional insights have been provided on some of those middle grade Union officers who when not fighting among themselves gave some stability to the Army of the Potomac. The views of Henry N. Blake, a whistle-blowing roundhead junior officer who called it the way he saw it, are brought into focus. Blake knew he had a losing hand from a legal standpoint, but this did not deter him from working tirelessly for the defense from his jail cell. This chess playing intellectual's narrative has been ignored by many historians. It is suggested that his highly negative views of General Carr should not be summarily dismissed on the basis of possible personal bias. Perhaps his standards for a brigade commander were unrealistically high, for even where Carr stood at Chancellorsville or Gettysburg it was very dangerous, but these were the standards Blake and most veteran soldiers believed were appropriate for the Hooker Brigade.

Undoubtedly Blake's early and fearless attacks on some of the sacred cows of the time did not enhance his popularity through his published work in 1865. Later in life, he wrote that he should have postponed the writing of his book until the official reports were available. But much can be said for his relatively contemporaneous telling of his story, unaffected by subsequent study of other versions—revisionist or otherwise—of the events described. His somewhat vaguely expressed reservations about Andrew A. Humphreys lead to a deeper examination of Humphreys' military career, and some aspects of his personality and military record are highlighted which were not dealt with by his biographer, his son and aide, Henry Humphreys, and other commentators.

A little more light has been shed on the life of William Blaisdell who, it can be argued, should be accorded accolades equal to those of his distinguished antagonist, Robert McAllister. Mother McAllister and Old Cruelty make an interesting contrast, as do the Harvard "abolitionist" Blake and the Harvard "copperhead" Abbott. But these men of differing views on politics and social behavior shared an extraordinary dedication to duty.

Abbott and Blake also shared an all too common burden in the Civil War—the loss of a brother. William E. Blake, 18 years old when he enlisted in Company K with his older brother, was worn down by First Bull Run, the Peninsula, and Second Bull Run and died of disease at Falmouth on December 21, 1863. Henry Blake at the time was just returning with Company K from the battle of Fredericksburg. Colonel Blaisdell showed courage and compassion when the army would not give Henry Blake leave to accompany his brother's body back to Boston and told Blake, who had not been home in eighteen months, to go without orders, that he would cover for him. The AWOL Blake was instructed to come right back if it appeared that a campaign was imminent. He scrupulously obeyed this instruction and in just over a week was back in time to participate in the infamous Mud March.(288)

Henry Abbott was the third brother in the war. He described himself as the least military of the Abbotts to enlist. His elder brother, Edward, and his younger brother, Fletcher, enlisted in the 2nd Massachusetts at about the same time that the Blakes enlisted in the 11th Massachusetts. Unlike the Blakes, they entered as a captain and second lieutenant, respectively. Edward was killed at Cedar Mountain in August, 1862; Fletcher survived the war.(289)

The trial transcripts do not give us much more insight how such men of great physical courage as Alexander Hays or Henry Abbott weighed the evidence of insubordination against the alleged cowardice of the man who brought the charges.

The relationships between the higher ranking generals—Meade, Hancock, Humphreys, Birney and Carr—are examined to a limited degree and certain hypotheses to explain their actions are put forth. The actions of other Hooker Brigade regimental commanders in addition to

Russell Blood

Pvt. Samuel Blood, known as Uncle Sam in his later years, dressed in his GAR uniform.

Blaisdell and McAllister—Lieutenant Colonel Waldo Merriam, 16th Massachusetts; Colonel Napoleon Bonaparte McLoughlen, 1st Massachusetts; and Lieutenant Colonel John Schoonhover, 11th New Jersey—whose names frequent the official records, are somewhat more revealed from both a military action standpoint and as to their roles in camp intrigue and clique formation. Much mystery still remains, however.

The brief military career of Private Samuel L. Blood in the Wilderness is a reminder of what all too often happens to the "replacement" infantry soldiers in our longer wars. His experience was repeated many times in World War II, Korea and Viet Nam. He was gone before they knew he was there. Private Blood, however, did at least have a month with the regiment while, as Blake noted after the first day of the Wilderness, "some of the recruits, who joined their commands about forty-eight hours before the army evacuated its winter quarters, were slain in this encounter."(290) Although after Bull Run there were probably never many more than thirty privates in Company K at any one time, there were about 160 privates listed as mustered in the company during the war.

Private Blood was in Army hospitals and convalescent facilities for over a year after the Wilderness and finally was discharged on July 25, 1865. After the war he taught school in Billerica, Massachusetts, and married a fellow school teacher in 1869. They moved to Chicago about 1870, where he worked in the post office. In 1871 Mrs. O'Leary's cow tried to reenact the conflagration of the Wilderness, and as a result, the couple lost all their belongings in the great Chicago fire. The Bloods returned to his family farm in Chelmsford, Massachusetts, where his wife died in 1875, leaving him with two small children. In later life he moved to Lowell and Saugus, Massachusetts, and operated a photography and notions shop. He died on January 2, 1925, in Saugus, where he lived with his son, my uncle. To the children in the neighborhood he was known as "Uncle Sam."(291)

The Last Meeting of the Hooker Brigade

The largest of all of the Civil War reunions was the 50th, held at Gettysburg in 1913. Nearly all of the protagonists at the Brandy Station courts martial were dead, and none were mentioned by Henry Blake, who organized the meeting of the Hooker Brigade. Blake, who had returned to Massachusetts from Montana around the turn of the century, wrote in his memoirs:

An association of the survivors of First Brigade, Second Division, III Corps, Army of the Potomac [the Hooker Brigade] was formed during the winter and a lease was secured about six months before the reunion, of private property comprising the site of Peter Roger's house and barn, within their lines in battle. A very small part of the old house, where the women baked bread for the soldiers, is attached to the modern building two stories high. . . . The Governors of Alabama, Florida and Mississippi were requested to designate two members of the respective regiment from their states which assaulted our position, July 2nd, 1863. There was a substantial compliance with this request and these representative of our foes were treated as our guests.

While arrangements were being made in Boston, Gen. Sickles, formerly in command of the III Corps, telegraphed his wish to be guest of the Brigade and pay his share of the expenses, and a room was provided for him. The widow of Gen. Longstreet, his second wife, was

MOLLUS-USAMHI

Generals Joseph Carr, Daniel Sickles and Charles Graham (from left) at a GAR reunion at Gettysburg in the 1880s.

also a sharer of our hospitality on the same conditions. There were ten or more Confederates from Alabama and Mississippi who were entertained during the reunion but I cannot recall any from Florida. The memories of the combat were revived and manifold tales were unfolded. One of our antagonists from Alabama said, "When I crossed the Emmitsburg road and saw your troops, I raised my eyes to heaven and exclaimed, O Lord if you will only permit me to walk safely from this field, I will serve thee as long as I live." He redeemed his promise and was a Baptist preacher over fifty years. . . . General Sickles was a big drawing card and more old soldiers, both Union and Confederate, called to pay their respects to him than any other person there. . . . The stump of one leg lost in this battle was about three inches long and the Gen. sat most of the time in his chair, from which he could see the place where he was wounded. . . .

He exchanged greeting with thousands and his friends cautioned him against over exertion, but he answered uniformly, "Where could I die in a better place than in this spot?"(292)

National Archives

General Sickles and the Hooker Brigade at the Rogers House during the 1913 reunion at Gettysburg. Sickles is in the chair at center. Henry Blake is the eighth veteran from the left.

General Sickles had not lost his sense of humor. Blake wrote:

> He was introduced to a group, claiming to have followed Pickett in his famous charge and shouted, "There's a mistake about this, I have already seen more men than were under Pickett, and there must have been some who were killed."(293)

In writing of the reunion, Blake presented his view and that of his fellow veterans on Sickles' controversial action in moving the III Corps forward at Gettysburg on the second day. Also, not surprisingly, he registered a rebuke to General Meade, mild compared to those in his book, for his lack of action after Gettysburg:

> The weight of military critics is against the correctness of the advance of the III Corps on July 2nd, 1863, and it is styled a serious blunder, but the combatants who risked their lives fighting for and against the Union forces stand by Sickles. The view of the soldiers is embodied in the

remark, reported to have been made by President Lincoln. "Gen., you are charged with provoking an attack with the enemy, you don't need a court of inquiry to find you guilty." The fact that Sickles was ready to lead his command wherever it was ordered to go covered his military sins. . . .

In conversations with the Confederates, the opinion was unanimous that the pursuit of our enemy should have been more persistent and the earthworks of our enemy could have been carried with slight loss. They lacked ammunition and articles indispensable in war, but the Union Generals were not informed concerning the real conditions of the enemy and a great opportunity was lost.(294)

Blake erred in accusing Sickles of exaggerating his age, "saying he was in his ninetieth year." Actually it was an understatement, not a common Sickles trait, as Sickles was ninety-four years old at the time. He died within the year, on May 4, 1914, at age ninety-five. The *New York Times* obituary was also understated, declaring that "He was truly an adventurous spirit."(295)

Henry Blake, when he wrote about the reunion, could not know that he was going to rival Sickles for longevity. He lived for twenty more years in Boston and was the oldest survivor of the Harvard Law School at the time of his death and, perhaps, of the 11th Massachusetts and the Hooker Brigade.

The *New York Times* (November 29, 1933) headlines on the obituary for the 95-year-old Blake were, in descending order:

H. N. Blake Dead; Retired Jurist
Last Territorial Chief Justice of Montana and
First Under Statehood
Served in Civil War
With Bride Rode 400 Miles in Stage Coach to
Post in Days of Indian Uprisings

With Henry Blake's death, the book was closed on the Brandy Station courts martial.

Appendix A: Veteran III Corps Units Before and After Reorganization on March 25, 1864

III CORPS	NEW II CORPS
FIRST DIVISION (BIRNEY)	***THIRD DIVISION (BIRNEY)***

III CORPS

FIRST DIVISION (BIRNEY)

First Brigade (Collis)
57th, 63rd, 105th, 110th
and 141st Pennsylvania

Second Brigade (Ward)
20th Indiana, 3rd and 4th Maine,
6th and 104th New York,
99th Pennsylvania and
2nd U.S. Sharpshooters

Third Brigade (Egan)
17th Maine, 3rd and 5th Michigan,
40th New York, 68th Pennsylvania
and 1st U.S. Sharpshooters

SECOND DIVISION (PRINCE)

First Brigade (Blaisdell)
1st, 11th & 16th Massachusetts,
11th New Jersey and
26th and 84th Pennsylvania

Second Brigade (Brewster)
70th, 71st, 72nd, 73rd, 74th
and 120th New York

Third Brigade (Mott)
5th, 6th, 7th and 8th New Jersey
and 115th New York

NEW II CORPS

THIRD DIVISION (BIRNEY)

First Brigade (Ward)
20th Indiana, 3rd Maine,
40th, 86th and 124th New York,
99th, 110th and 141st Pennsylvania
and 2nd U.S. Sharpshooters

Second Brigade (Hays)
4th and 17th Maine, 3rd and 5th
Michigan, 93rd New York,
57th, 63rd and 105th Pennsylvania
and 1st U.S. Sharpshooters

***FOURTH DIVISION
(CARR-MOTT)***

First Brigade (McAllister)
1st and 16th Massachusetts,
5th, 6th, 7th, 8th and 11th New Jersey,
26th and 115th Pennsylvania

Second Brigade (Brewster-Blaisdell)
70th, 71st, 72nd, 74th and 120th New
York, 84th Pennsylvania
and 11th Massachusetts

On May 13, 1864, the Fourth Div., II corps, was disbanded and incorporated into the Third Division. The First Brigade (McAllister) became Third Brigade (Mott) and Second Brigade (Brewster) became Fourth Brigade (Brewster) of the Third Division. The Third Division, III Corps, was not composed of veteran regiments at the time of the reorganization; it had been added after Gettysburg.

Appendix B: Post War Careers

Robert McAllister

General McAllister was mustered out of the service in June of 1865, and returned to Belvedere, New Jersey. A native of Pennsylvania, he had moved to New Jersey to pursue his railroad construction business a few years before the war. His first post-war business experience—a "part interest in a Mississippi cotton plantation—ended in financial ruin."(296) Shortly thereafter he was offered employment as the general manager of the Ironton Railroad, an ore mining and railroad operation based just across the Pennsylvania state line. A few years after the war, he reconciled with his elder brother, Pórter, who served with the South in a Virginia regiment, and who died soon after. Robert McAllister held his Ironton position until failing health in the 1880s forced his retirement. He died on February 23, 1891, at the age of seventy-seven.

Frederick B. Arner

Henry Harrison Bingham

The twenty-six-year-old general left the Army in 1866 and returned to Philadelphia to clerk for a prominent lawyer. In 1867, he was appointed postmaster of Philadelphia by President Andrew Johnson, upon the recommendation of generals Meade and Hancock. After five years in this position he ran successfully for clerk of courts in Philadelphia County, and then was elected to Congress as a Republican in 1879. He served in the House of Repre-

Henry Bingham's meeting with the dying Lewis Armistead after Pickett's charge is honored in this Masonic memorial at Gettysburg, dedicated in 1993. Bingham bore a message from the Confederate general to his pre-war friend, Winfield Scott Hancock, who lay seriously wounded nearby.

sentatives until his death on March 22, 1912.

Henry Blake wrote that he met Bingham in Chicago in 1880 at the Republican National Convention, where they were both delegates, "and exchanged friendly greetings and revived our experience."(297)

Bingham's tenure of more than thirty-three years earned him the title "Father of the House," in his later years he was the oldest member in continuous service. A perusal of his record shows him not to be what might be termed a brilliant legislator but probably a very effective member in serving the interests of his Philadelphia constituents. At one time he was chairman of the Committee on Post Offices and Post Roads and, according to his memorial tributes, was "instrumental in securing the reduction of letter postage from 3 to 2 cents and the rate on second-class mail matter from 2 cents to 1 cent a pound."(298) Bingham was a long time member of the Appropriations Committee and a candidate for the Speakership on a number of occasions.

Joseph B. Carr

General Carr became involved in the manufacturing of chains for cranes and dredges in his hometown of Troy, New York, and continued his participation in militia affairs, as he had done for more than ten years prior to the war. In 1867 he was appointed major-general of the Third Division of the New York State Militia. He commanded the militia in 1877 in putting down some railroad strike riots and "dispersed a mob in Albany without firing a shot."(299)

Carr was also actively involved in Republican politics and was elected secretary of state of New York in 1879. He was re-elected in 1881 and 1883, but was the unsuccessful Republican candidate for lieutenant governor in 1885. He died in Troy on February 24, 1895.

Henry N. Blake

When he went west in 1866, Blake took the train to St. Louis and from there embarked on a steamboat, formerly used by the army, up the Missouri River. Blake wrote that at Fort Benton he and five other persons

162

hired a freighter . . . to transport us to Helena, 150 miles distant. . . . We escaped prowling savages and horse thieves and were in a city barely two years old.(300)

Blake went on to Virginia City, about 100 miles from Helena. He noted that things were not quite like Boston.

What was a felony in Massachusetts with severe penalties was tolerated and protected in Montana. Nearly every man carried a revolver or weapon for ready use and gun plays were common affairs. It was evident at a glance that liquor dealers, gamblers and what is known as the sporting element held the balance of power in the town.(301)

Blake first tried prospecting after inspecting "miners at work with sluice boxes in Alder Gulch and cleaning up fine gold."

I hired a log cabin with a roof of dirt on the north side of the city and was crazy to try my luck in mining. . . . I worked ten days on old claims in the Fairweather district, during which the miners held a meeting and I was chosen secretary of the organization.(302)

Blake reported that he "gained wisdom but no money." He then was offered more suitable employment as a substitute for the ailing editor of the Montana Post. The newspaper was published in Virginia City and also covered Helena news. The editor eventually died, and Blake became the permanent editor. He wrote of his experience:

I made friends as well as enemies in my editorial career and associated with the prominent citizens of the territory and acquired a style of ready if not brilliant composition, which was beneficial in my entire life in Montana and Massachusetts since my return. The preparations of the locals for the tri-weekly edition was troublesome because there was a paucity in the county tributary to a village as small as Virginia City, and mountains were made of molehills, dressed to the best of my ability in attractive phrases.(303)

He had been in town only two weeks when he was asked to join the Vigilantes, which Blake said "was virtually a certificate of an investigation and finding I was of good moral character."(304) He said the Vigilantes were in the process of ending their law and order activities "with the opening of the courts and the reign of law." Blake did not attend any meetings but corrected the proof on the "History of the Vigilantes," which recorded their activities. The tone of the work is evident from the following sample:

A butcher . . . received fifty lashes and was banished from the territory for stealing a calf. A married man was banished for mistreating his wife. A person was hung in the spring of 1867 near Virginia City to a tripod of fence rails for being a spy and reporting to confederates in Idaho the dates when the treasure coaches left the Territory. A small piece of paper on which I read the significant word "Vigilantes" was pinned on the back of his coat.(305)

Blake noted that the population was supported by gold mining and, not surprisingly, lacked some stability.

Few persons except fugitives from justice or domestic troubles expected to remain permanently in this region and the majority hoped to make his "steal" and return to his early home. Confederate soldiers and friends from the border states, . . . and exiles running away from the draft in the north, controlled the political situation. . . . The delegate to Congress and most of the members of the Legislative Assembly were Democrats of this species, when Lincoln was striving to preserve the Union. Families from the north were rare, and I attended a dance in Virginia City where there were twelve women and fifty men.(306)

Blake was a Republican editing a Republican newspaper, and this brought him into conflict with the Democrats and the Montana power structure. The latter was in the person of the famous leader of the Irish Brigade, General Thomas Francis Meagher. Unlike General Carr, Meagher was no Irish dancing master. Blake wrote,

I gained notoriety beyond the Rocky Mountains by a controversy with General Meagher, who was Secretary of the Territory, and Acting Governor in the absence of that official. His public life as an orator, soldier and idol of his countrymen are well known and my comments will be confined to his acts as a resident of Montana. He had an excessive

164

bump of vanity, was fond of seeing his name in a halo of praise, and his office in Virginia City was thronged with a gang of bibulous politicians and flatterers who promised to send him to Congress.(307)

Blake quoted Joaquin Miller's *History of Montana:*

Of course Meagher was about the last person in the land to be at the head of offices in Montana; he was utterly unsuited for such an office; Meagher seemed only fitted to fight.(308)

The issue precipitating the conflict was whether the governor had the power to authorize an election for a legislative assembly or whether only Congress could do so. Meagher had ruled both ways but had finally come down supporting the Democratic position that the governor could authorize an election. The Republicans maintained that the subsequent elections of the second and third legislatures were null and void.

Blake admitted a little Puritan bias in that "I was acquainted with the reputation of Gen. Meagher and his associates in the army for sobriety." He wrote that Meagher "did not read high sounding enconiums from my pen and what I did write respecting him was true."(309)

In October of 1866 Meagher took umbrage at a squib in the paper, demanded an apology, and threatened to challenge the publisher of the paper to a duel if a retraction was not forthcoming. Blake informed Meagher that he, not the publisher, "was responsible and ready to correct any mistake, but would not be a party to a duel."(310)

Blake wrote that he got a written challenge, and

on the same day I sent a reply. I printed both letters in *The Post* under the heading, "Pistols and Coffee for Two." The original challenge is in my possession, and there was no further correspondence between us, and I was not posted as a coward or assailed in any manner.(311)

The following spring (1867) General Meagher rather surprisingly appointed Blake a colonel and assistant adjutant of a mounted regiment to fight the current Indian War. Blake wrote that this "was *prima facie* evidence that he did not entertain any malice towards me though there had not been any personal intercourse." The commander of the expedition was a former Confederate colonel, Thomas Thoroughman. Blake noticed some differences between the

11th Massachusetts "and the mob with which I was enrolled." He noted that "there were no roll calls or drills on any pretense of discipline. My suggestions of their necessity and importance were ignored."(312)

The action was hardly a war, since it was mainly conducted against Indians stealing horses. Subsequently it was learned that no Indian outbreak had been planned in the first place, but that the people, knowing the massacres of the past, had called for protection.

After seven weeks, Blake's second military career ended. He turned in his government horse and his exulted rank. This was really a volunteer service in that they received no pay. Blake did not comment on how he and his horse got along, considering his expressed aversion to such beasts in his early life and in the army.

Blake tactfully did not mention the circumstances of General Meagher's demise. On July 1, 1867, during a drunken spree at Fort Benton, Montana, he presumably fell from the deck of a steamboat into the Missouri River under mysterious circumstances. His body was not recovered.(313)

In 1867 Henry Blake, now 28 years old, resumed his practice of law. He observed, "I reflected on the remark of my friend, Richard H. Dana, in 1859, 'A lawyer is young until he is thirty and has ample time to prepare for the work of his profession.'"(314)

His library included the Statutes of Montana (one volume), Blackstone's *Commentaries* and a book of forms. His first assignment was to prepare a constitution and by-laws for the Typographical Union, which when duly organized immediately called a strike against the Montana *Democrat*. Speaking as a life–long Republican, Blake stated that

like most strikes the demands of the workmen were unreasonable, the *Democrat* was not making any money, and within two years (the paper) expired.(315)

In 1869 his career took a crucial turn when he was named the U.S. attorney for the territory by the newly elected president, U. S. Grant. He said he had taken no steps to procure the position.(316)

Shortly after this appointment, Blake went back to Boston to press his suit of marriage to Miss Clara Jane Clark. It was about time, since he had written his original proposal in 1866. His grandson added a footnote to the story, reporting that Miss Clark greeted her suitor at the front walk in Boston with the words, "I will not marry you, Henry Blake." Blake responded with a twinkle in his eye, "Why don't you wait until you are asked?"(317) They were married in Boston in January and returned to Virginia City in the spring of 1870. They settled, Blake noted, in a house occupied previously by an Englishman by the name of William Shakespeare.

Blake was appointed a district attorney for the First Judicial District of the territorial government, which did a brisker business than the U.S. attorney's office. He was re-elected and served in that post until 1873. Blake was also the reporter for the Montana supreme court on volume one of its records and assisted with volumes two and three.

After visiting Boston in the winter of 1873-1874, he and his wife

MOLLUS-USAMHI
Montana Supreme Court Justice Henry N. Blake.

returned to Montana with the first authentic Yankee baked bean pot used there. Blake purchased a third interest in the *Montanian* newspaper and immediately embarked on an unsuccessful but determined campaign to make Virginia City the capital of Montana rather than Helena. As a result of his editorial efforts he was elected to the Montana legislative assembly in 1874 but lost his position as supreme court reporter. He observed that

> the editor who plunges into the battle of words, regardless of consequences, makes zealous friends and savage enemies. This was my fate, but I have decided to exclude from these pages every tale of bribery an corruption relating to the capital of Montana from first to last. I could "a tale unfold," but won't.(318)

Politically weak in Helena, Blake seemed strong in Washington, and in 1875 President Grant appointed him to the supreme court of the Montana Territory, where he served until 1880. Blake said his humble law library was augmented to a great degree, which was a financial mistake, but "a judge without the authorities is like a mechanic without tools."(319) He was elected to the

167

legislature and served during 1880, 1882 and 1886. In 1884 he was again elected as district attorney, and in March 1889 he was appointed chief justice of the supreme court of the territory. At this point his twenty-three year residence in Virginia City ended, and he moved to Helena. In November of that year Montana became a state, and Blake was elected the first chief justice. He served until 1892, when he was defeated for re-election and returned to private practice. In 1897 he was appointed master of chancery for the state and tried a number of important cases.

The Blakes returned to Boston in 1910 and spent more than twenty years together there before they died. Judge Blake died on November 29, 1933, at age 95. His wife had died one year earlier, on the same date. The *Boston Herald* (Nov. 30) noted that at age 14 he was a member of the first class to enter Dorchester High School, and at his death was the oldest graduate of the Harvard Law School.(320)

Appendix C: The Battle of the Boydton Plank Road

The Boydton Plank Road battle was the most difficult engagement for the 11th Massachusetts after most of its veterans had returned to Boston in June 1864. A number of participants in the Brandy Station courts martial played prominent and, in a number of cases, tragic roles in the battle. The regiment, the sole surviving unit of the original Hooker brigade, and the 11th New Jersey were considered by their brigade commander, Colonel McAllister, to be his most battle-tested and dependable regiments. The battle, where the 11th Massachusetts lost two of its veteran officers, had elements of confusion and misadventure similar to the Wilderness. The battle was significant to McAllister in that it finally got him his brigadier's star.

This engagement on October 27 was one of the last attempts by Union forces to break the stalemate at Petersburg in the fall of 1864. General Andrew Humphreys described the terrain involved, which was south and west of Petersburg:

> The country over which it extended was very imperfectly known to us, and was as densely wooded as the Wilderness. Owing to these facts our troops and officers got strangely mixed at times, their staff officer riding into our lines and even into some of the Headquarters at times, mistaking them for their own, and ours doing the same.(321)

The battle that ensued was the result of an abortive attempt to flank the Confederate defenses around Petersburg and cut the Southside Railroad. Nothing went well, with the V Corps, under General Gouveneur Warren, bogging down in a forest and being unable to link up with Hancock's II Corps divisions. The McAllister Brigade was temporarily attached to the Second Division (now under Thomas W. Egan) and was attacked through the gap between the two corps by Confederate General Henry Heth's Division of A. P. Hill's III Corps.

Lieutenant W.H. Wheeler, one of the five officers and 166 enlisted men who came to the 11th when the 16th Massachusetts enlistments expired, described the action.

MOLLUS-USAMHI

Captain Alexander McTavish, 11th Massachusetts

[The regiment] marched about eight miles to Boydton plank road, formed a line of battle on the crest of a hill when the enemy commenced firing in our rear. We about faced and charged down the hill and up another where we met the enemy. Our loss in this engagement was one commissioned officer Capt. [Daniel] Granger who was mortally wounded and left on the field, one enlisted man killed and eight wounded and twelve missing, supposed to have been wounded and left on the field. The command fell back and reformed on the hill, our loss in this move was one enlisted man killed and one officer, Captain Alexander McTavish. McTavish took command of the Regiment after Capt. Granger was wounded. At this time the highest officer in rank, Major Charles C. Rivers, was not with us, being division officer of the day. . . . Capt. McTavish and myself were sitting down talking with our backs toward what in the beginning was our front, when at once there was a dull thud and he fell over backwards and was dead being shot through the heart. . . . We had to leave him on the field for it was all we could do to get away ourselves being nearly surrounded. After Capt. McTavish was killed I took command and commanded the Regiment until the following afternoon when Major Rivers joined us and took command.(322)

Alexander McTavish and Henry Blake had both been wounded at Spotsylvania and returned to Boston together from a convalescent hospital at Annapolis. Blake wrote in his memoirs:

I was disabled by my wound from serving within three months and advised earnestly First Lieutenant McTavish, who was mustered with the 11th and hesitating concerning his course, that I wished to take my place as Captain in the Battalion. I assured him I would go back if my health was restored and bade him good bye at the station of the Old Colony in Boston when he departed for the Army of the Potomac. He perished in the first battle after his assignment to duty. Was my life saved under these circumstances?(323)

A few days after the battle Colonel McAllister wrote a long letter to his family describing the Plank Road expedition.

I was then ordered to extend my left with the rear line of battle, making but one line. I had just completed this, preparatory to taking the opposite hill, when we were all surprised at the roar of musketry and artillery in our rear. The two Brigades of my Division under Genl. Mott were attacked. Our ambulances and artillery were all exposed and liable to be captured. These had to be protected. These Brigades had to change front and fight the enemy on the very road we had just come in on. This left our rear and the plank road exposed, and the enemy pushed right up towards us on the hill. A few minutes more and we could be surrounded. . . . We had secured the road, and the V Corps was to have connected with us. This they had failed to do. The enemy's column passed through the gap thus left. And what was still worse, we had no ammunition except sixty rounds to a man in the cartridge boxes and on the persons of the men. We were to have received a new supply of ammunition along the line from the V Corps, but the want of a connection prevented this. . . .

Genl. Egan ordered me to about face and charge the enemy. I gave the order, and off on the charge we went—down the hill, through the hazel brush and swamp. We met the enemy, drove them back pell mell, and captured over 100 prisoners. We met a heavy fire from two brigades in our rear (of which we knew nothing). This and the enemy's fire on my left—now the right—were too severe for my new troops. My line faltered and broke as we rose up the hill on the opposite side. . . . The enemy, encouraged by our falling back, re-attacked. My men opened on them with a terrific fire and drove them back once more. The day was ours. Our communication was opened and the enemy passed from our rear. . . . The charge not only saved Egan's Division and my Brigade, but saved the Corps. Just as we were making it, the enemy was planting a battery in my rear (now my front). . . . The darkness of the night closed in around us. A few pickets firing, an occasional shot, was all that was left of the sound of battle. Stillness reigned throughout the field. The rain poured down rapidly. The men lay down on the cold, wet ground and fell fast asleep.(324)

In a strange coincidence, Judge Advocate Bingham on Hancock's staff had been sent off during the late afternoon to try to find the V Corps (Samuel W. Crawford's Division) and get them to close the gap that General Heth was so ably exploiting. Major Bingham not only did not find Crawford but was captured by the Confederates. He was able to escape later in the evening, but the contact with the V Corps was never established.(325)

Colonel McAllister reported on the last hours of Captain Granger and the difficult position of the wounded generally after the battle.

On the plank road stood two houses. Here our wounded were carried—those that were taken back. With an aide I rode and called to see them. In one house were 50 men from my Brigade. They were badly wounded, many of them mortally. In another house were about a dozen more. Poor fellows. They would take me by the hand and say,"Colonel, did I do my duty?"

"Yes! Yes!" I would reply. "You did it nobly. You did it nobly."

They would say "I fought for my country, and I die for my country."

Oh, how my heart thrilled for these poor, dying soldiers! They were far from home and friends; and they were soon to be left in the hands of the enemy, for our ambulances were but few and all full. The ambulances could not make a second trip, and our part of the battlefield was so far in the advance—right in on the enemy.

Only one Surgeon made his appearance at these hospital houses. There were no nurses, no chaplains, no consolation, no relief. There was hardly a candle to light up the rooms even while we were there to see the wounded. Capt. Granger, an old veteran captain and a brave and gallant officer, commanded the 11th Massachusetts that day. He fell mortally wounded and was lying on the floor of one of the houses, suffering intense pain. He was so anxious to be taken to the ambulances that I ordered his regiment to carry him and as many others as they could down to the ambulances, about a mile distant. We had not stretchers, and it was pitch dark and raining. Some were carried some were not. Some died while being carried. On arriving at the designated place, they found the ambulances gone. The wounded had to be left. Capt. Granger died.

I had the greatest regard for him. He was so brave, so gallant, and he always did his duty. He belonged to the same regiment that Capt. Lombard does. . . . I shall never forget that day or that battle—surrounded on all sides, cut off from the balance of our Corps, no connection with the V Corps. The victorious yells of the Rebels sounded in our ears. Our fate seemed to be sealed without hope of escape. It was a time of suspense and doubt.(326)

About 10 P.M. of this very long day McAllister was ordered to withdraw from his position and to report back to General Mott. General Hancock had decided to withdraw the II Corps from its exposed position. He called in General DeTrobriand and put him in charge of the pickets and the cavalry to cover the second and third divisions' pull out. The operation was successfully carried out and in the morning the Confederates found "only the ashes of our extinguished fires." DeTrobriand wrote that at "seven o'clock in the morning, we had rejoined the division, and I reported to General Hancock the withdrawal of the pickets without fight or accident. This good result was due in great part to the active and earnest efforts of Colonel Rivers, commanding the 11th Massachusetts, who was on duty as officer of the day of the division."(327)

Appendix D: General Andrew A. Humphreys and General Joseph B. Carr—An Odd But Close Relationship

There is considerable evidence that General Andrew Humphreys, as Meade's chief of staff, served as a "guardian angel" to Joseph Carr. He must have played an instrumental role in Carr's appointment as commander of the Third Division, III Corps in the fall of 1863 and his subsequent appointment to the Fourth Division, II Corps in March 1864. The latter appointment was made even though Carr's record at Mine Run was marginal and he lacked Senate confirmation. Humphreys and Meade apparently tried to keep Carr as a division commander. McAllister wrote that Carr would not accept command of a brigade.(328) If the Troy newspaper is to be believed, Humphreys played a major role in Carr's long-delayed Senate confirmation.(329) Humphreys' admiration for Carr is difficult to explain. They were, indeed, an odd couple.

General Humphreys

Andrew Humphreys was a "scientist" officer and a charter member of the National Academy of Science. During the Mexican War, he served as assistant topographical officer in charge of the Coast Survey Office in Washington, and in the 1850s had a succession of engineering and survey assignments. He was the chief topographical officer on General McClellan's staff from late 1861 until August 1862 and was appointed a brigadier general of volunteers in April 1862. In August he was given his first command, a new division of the V Corps. At Fredericksburg, after 30 years in the army, Humphreys finally got his chance to see action, and it seemed to convince him that this was his real calling. Humphreys wrote his wife:

The charge of my division [at the stone wall at the base of Marye's Heights] is described by those who witnessed it as sublime, and H[enry, his son and aide] tells me, that he heard some general officers who saw it (who did not know him) discussing it, and saying that it was the grandest sight they ever saw, and that as I led the charge and bared my head, raising my right arm to heaven, the setting sun shining full upon my face gave me the aspect of an inspired being.

This is quite egotistical, is it not? I felt gloriously, and as the storm of bullets whistled around me, and as the shells and shrapnel burst close to me in every direction scattering with hissing sound their fragments and bullets, the excitement grew more glorious still.

Library of Congress
General Andrew A. Humphreys

Oh, it was sublime! As we neared the enemy's works their lines became a sheet of flame that enveloped us in front and flank. We advanced to within thirty yards of them. Nearly our whole loss occurred in the charge and retiring, which occupied each brigade from ten to fifteen minutes, and in that time I lost more than 1,000 officers and men. In all I was exposed to their fire an hour and a half, being about one hundred and fifty yards from them, but the officers and men were under partial shelter except when charging and retiring.(330)

His new-found enthusiasm for military combat was also evident in a letter to a friend.

I felt like a young girl of sixteen at her first ball; I felt more like a god than a man; I now understand what Charles XII meant when he said, "Let the whistling of bullets hereafter be my music."(331)

The Mud March, somewhat less exhilarating, followed in January 1863, and Humphreys' division was not heavily engaged at Chancellorsville. In May the division was broken up, and he was assigned to the Second Division, III Corps. He wrote:

I am going to the Headquarters of the Army to receive orders for my new command, which it is settled shall be Hooker's old division, one of the best in the whole army. . . . I understand General Hooker himself has done this; complimentary certainly, and to tell you the truth, the command of an old Division of old troops promises much less labor than I have had for the past eight months. . . . It is acknowledged throughout this army that no officer ever did as much with troops of short term of service as I have done with these, and it is acknowledged at the same time that no one else would or could have done as much.(332)

Humphreys believed he was still suffering from his "scientist" image, and he did not think that his accomplishments in the V Corps and at Fredericksburg had been fully appreciated. He wrote, "Why, anyone who knows me intimately, knows that I had more of the soldier than a man of science in me."(333)

On the march to Gettysburg, right after Meade's assumption of command of the Army of the Potomac, Humphreys was offered the position of chief of staff. He either declined or deferred it, and Meade wrote that the two agreed that "General Humphreys could be of greater service by retaining command of his division in the III Corps during the impending battle."(334)

After Gettysburg, Meade again offered him the position, along with a commission as a major general. Although he accepted it on July 8, 1863, Humphreys again asserted his desire to command troops.

I prefer infinitely the command of troops to this position of Chief of Staff. It suits me in nothing, my habits, my wishes, my tastes. It is even more distasteful to me than I can well express and I feel these depressed at no longer commanding.

Everyone appears to regard it so differently. I hate to be second to anyone. However, at the first opportunity I shall leave it, and if necessary to do so will send back my Major General's Commission, and take the Brigadier General. I cannot bear to be without command.(335)

But these words belie subsequent events, as Humphreys served as Meade's chief of staff for fifteen more months. A somewhat changed attitude toward his job was evident by the summer of 1863:

When I think how much depends upon this army of the Potomac, I recognized that the command of it is the most important command in the

176

country, and the position of Chief of Staff is no mean place in that army; . . . I prefer command of course, but hardly the command of a division.(336)

When he had moved the Army of the Potomac across the Rapidan in May of 1864, he reported that he was "depressed" about the situation that he and General Meade had been placed in, observing that if the campaign was a success, General Grant would get the credit; but if it was a failure, Meade and he would get blamed. He wrote,

[A]s soon as we get in motion the excitement of action will drive it (the depression) all off. . . . I made a mistake in accepting this position of Chief of Staff and I am vexed at myself for doing it. I have not had a cheerful professional feeling since, except when the Army got into tight places. It has been almost unendurable to me at times.(337)

His son wrote of his father during the spring offensive of May-June 1864.

At times he went among the soldiers or made personal investigations, but as a rule remained at his desk receiving and sending dispatches.(338)

And when the opportunity finally came to command a corps, it turned out that it would not be just any corps. In mid July, 1864, Grant wrote to Meade suggesting that Humphreys be offered the command of the X Corps. Grant pointed out that it would eventually be composed of one-half colored troops, and said he did "not suppose this would make any difference in General Humphreys performance of his duties, but it might have something to do with his preference for the command."(339)

Humphreys wrote that he prepared a note to Grant

to thank him for his kind consideration in the matter, and explaining that the character, the reputation, the honor of the troops I commanded were part of my own, that the two were so closely connected that they could not be separated, and that I could not have such feeling for any other than my own race and my own people, and that therefore I preferred not to command the corps he mentioned.(340)

The actual draft of the note stated:

while I have the kindliest feelings for the negro race and gladly see everything done that promises to ameliorate their condition, yet as they are not my own people, nor my own race, I could not feel toward negro troops as I have always felt toward the troops I have commanded.(341)

He never sent the note, however, because he heard the X Corps had been given to General David Birney on July 23rd. Although both Humphreys and Birney were from Philadelphia, their attitude toward colored troops was quite different. Birney led the X Corps in mid August in the Deep Bottom expedition. On August 19, 1864, he reported:

The enemy attacked my line in heavy force last night, and was repulsed with great loss. In front of one colored regiment, eighty-two dead bodies are counted. The colored troops behaved handsomely and are in fine spirits.(342)

And in a general order the same day Birney congratulated the X Corps on its performance:

It has on each occasion, when ordered, broken the enemy's strong lines, and has captured during this short campaign four siege guns, protected by the most formidable works, six strands of colors, and many prisoners. . . . To the colored troops, recently added to us and fighting with us, the major-general commanding tenders his thanks for their uniform good conduct and soldierly bearing, setting a good example to our veterans, by the entire absence of straggling on the march.(343)

The troops reciprocated his kind words by saying that the initials D. B. in his name stood for Deep Bottom. He was affectionately called Deep Bottom Birney by the soldiers in his corps for the remaining three months of his life.(344)

On November 26, 1864, Humphreys replaced Hancock as commander of the all white II Corps. In the waning months of the war, the bullets very occasionally whizzed above his head as he led his corps to Appomattox Court House.

Humphreys had a reputation of a martinet which would fit in with Blake's description of the Gettysburg marches, where he and Carr were presented as collaborators. Lieutenant Colonel Theodore Lyman wrote:

[Humphreys] is most easy to get on with, for everybody; but, practically, he is just as hard as the Commander (Meade), for he had a tremendous temper, a great idea of military duty, and is very particular. When he does get wrathy, he sets his teeth and lets go a torrent of adjectives that must rather astonish those not used to little outbursts.(345)

Lyman, of course, observed him only as Meade's chief of staff.

General Carr

In stark contrast to Humphreys, Carr had little formal education and no particular talent for writing. Blake went so far as to call him an ignoramus. And while Humphreys had a reputation as a "fighting up-front" general, Carr's performance and reputation seem to be somewhat lacking in this area. Nevertheless, Carr appears to have had the ability to impress his superiors (Hooker, Humphreys and Meade) for appointment and promotion purposes. He knew how to ingratiate himself to a commander.(346) Although it does not appear that Carr and Humphreys were together much during the second day at Gettysburg, except when they were both back on Cemetery Ridge after the retreat from the forward position, Carr wrote the following in his report.

I may be pardoned, perhaps, for referring in my report to the conspicuous courage and remarkable coolness of the brigadier-general commanding the division during this terrific struggle. His presence was felt by the officers and men, as the enthusiastic manner in which he was greeted will testify.(347)

He very likely was pardoned for this reference, for General Humphreys was very sensitive about descriptions of the performance of the Second Division and himself at Gettysburg. He objected in very strong terms to the proposed reports of generals Hancock and Birney on the battle of Gettysburg and was successful in getting both to change passages that he considered as slights.(348)

During the period of the Meade-Sickles vendetta, Carr may have seemed to Meade and Humphreys to be one of the more malleable of the III Corps officers and less likely to believe in the divinity of Kearny, Hooker and Sickles, and the "III Corps which always did everything."

Carr also had some highly developed social skills that may account for his favorable impression on Humphreys. They shared a common desire for the good life, as best this could be put into effect in the Army of Potomac at Brandy Station. It is possible that Carr's background as a dancing master even helped him in cultivating Humphreys in this area. The earlier description of Humphreys' social life at Brandy Station is somewhat supportive of this theory.

Although apparently defending Carr, there is little evidence that later in 1864, when there was a shortage of capable field commanders, that either Meade or Humphreys sought him out to lead troops in the field after he was confirmed. It is true that he was in other commands. These commands, however, had even more problems with the lack of veteran field commanders and apparently he neither applied nor was summoned.(349)

Notes

Pages 1-10

1. Hutchinson, Gustavus B., *A Narrative of the Formation and Services of the Eleventh Massachusetts,* 1893 (Boston:Alfred Mudge and Sons), pp. 18-21.
2. Blake, Henry N., "Tales by an Old Harvard Soldier", *Harvard Alumni Bulletin,* June 16, 1927, p. 1058 *(Hereinafter* Old Harvard Soldier) and re the Wide-Awakes, Ware, E.E., *Political Opinion in Massachusetts During Civil War and Reconstruction,* 1916, (Columbia University), p. 3
3. Robertson, James I., ed. *The Civil War Letters of General Robert M. McAllister* (New Brunswick, NJ: Rutgers University Press), p. 402 *(Hereinafter* McAllister Letters)
4. *Army and Navy Journal,* May 13, 1865, p. 596
5. Pfanz, Harry W. *Gettysburg, The Second Day,* 1987 (Chapel Hill: University of North Carolina Press) p. 45
6. McAllister Letters, footnote 54, p. 221
7. *Troy* (New York) *Daily Times,* June 15, 1865, p. 1 *(Hereinafter Daily Times)*
8. Blake, Henry N., *Three Years in the Army of the Potomac,* 1865 (Boston: Lee & Shepard), p. 274 *(Hereinafter* Blake)
9. *Ibid,* p. 166
10. McAllister Letters, p. 279
11. Blake, pp. 191-192
12. *War of the Rebellion: A Compilation of the Official Records of the Union and Confederate Armies,* (U.S. Government Printing Office) Vol 51, Part I, pp. 1051-1052 *(Hereinafter* OR)
13. Blake, p. 191
14. *Ibid,* pp. 192-193
15. Cudworth, Warren H., *History of the First Regiment (Massachusetts),* 1866 (Boston: Walker, Fuller and Co.) pp. 383-384 *(Hereinafter* Cudworth)

16. Bartlett, A.W., *History of the Twelfth Regiment, New Hampshire Volunteers,* 1897 (Concord, N.C. Evans, Printer), p. 113 *(Hereinafter* 12th NH)
17. Blake, pp. 194-195
18. Cudworth, p. 385
19. Cooper, Thomas V., "26th Pennsylvania Volunteer Infantry, Pennsylvania's Memorial Days", 1889 (Library of Congress). Unpaged manuscript. *(Hereinafter* Cooper)
20. 12th NH, p. 114
21. Blake, p. 197
22. *Ibid,* pp. 198-199
23. Cudworth, p. 386
24. Cooper
25. Haynes, Martin A., *A History of the Second Regiment, New Hampshire Volunteer Infantry,* 1896 (Manchester: C.F. Livingston, printer), pp.134-135. Haynes writes that Gen. Humphreys "can have full credit" for the affair since no other general would contest for the "honors" of this night's work.
26. Blake, p. 201
27. OR, Vol. 51, Part I, pp. 1060-1061
28. Krick, Robert, "Lee's Greatest Victory", *Civil War Chronicles,* Summer 1991. "...two miles in fifty minutes, then ten minutes' rest, then do it again, and again, and again." p. 29
29. OR, Vol. 27, Part I, p. 543
30. Blake, p. 200-201
31. Humphreys, Henry H., *Andrew Atkinson Humphreys, A Biography,* 1924 (Philadelphia: John C. Winston), p. 190 *(Hereinafter* Humphreys Biography)
32. OR, Vol. 27, Part I, p. 543
33. Blake, p. 203
34. *Ibid,* pp. 208-209
35. *Ibid,* p. 209
36. *Ibid,* pp. 209-210
37. *Ibid,* p. 210
38. *Ibid*
39. *Daily Times,* pp. 6-7
40. Blake, pp. 210-211
41. *Ibid,* pp. 212-213
42. *Ibid,* p. 215
43. *Ibid,* p. 217
44. *Ibid,* p. 232
45. *Ibid,* pp. 234-235

46. *Ibid*, pp. 232-233
47. National Archives, Judge Advocate General files
48. Blake, p. 233
49. *Ibid*, p. 257
50. DeTrobriand, Regis, *Four Years with the Army of the Potomac,* 1889 (Boston: Tichnor and Company), pp. 530-531 *(Hereinafter* DeTrobriand) Col. DeTrobriand, a First Division, III Corps brigade commander, discusses fairly extensively how French's drinking affected his performance.
51. Swanberg, W.A., *Sickles the Incredible,* 1956 (Gettysburg: Stan Clark Books), p. 233
52. Walker, Francis A., *History of the Second Army Corp,* 1887. (Charles Scribner), pp. 557-558 *(Hereinafter* Walker)
53. Blake, p. 240
54. *Ibid*, p. 260
55. McAllister Letters, p. 339
56. *Ibid*, p. 385
57. Marbaker, Thomas D., *History of the 11th New Jersey Volunteers,* 1898 (MacCrellish and Quigley), p. 152 *(Hereinafter* Marbaker)
58. DeTrobriand, pp. 707-708
59. McAllister letters, p. 4
60. Higginson, T.W., *Massachusetts in the War, Vol II* (Boston: Wright & Potter Printing Co.), no date, pp. 887-888. Also see Grant story, p. 141
61. Blake, Henry, unpublished memoirs in the possession of Patricia Ernsberger, Mill Valley, California, p. 62 *(Hereinafter* Blake Memoirs)
62. *Ibid*
63. Blake, p. 314
64. *Ibid*, p. 315
65. Blake Memoirs, pp. 60-61
66. *Ibid*
67. The editor of the McAllister letters relies on the *Official Records, Vol. 51, Part I,* pp. 1040-1041 to support his thesis. This OR, however, does not support such an assertion, since it is General Sickles' recommendation of Blaisdell for promotion to brigadier "for gallant and meritorious services in the battle and operation of the 1st, 2nd and 3rd of May 1863. Colonel Blaisdell has served with distinction and fidelity in all the campaigns of this army, and is an officer of great merit." There is also a Sickles letter in the AGO file which states that "for Brigadier in place of [Amiel Weeks] Whipple [killed at Chancellorsville] I have recommended Col. William Blaisdell —one of the best officers in the service—a soldier from boyhood."

    Sickles also recommended Birney for the major-general spot of Hiram Berry, who also was killed at Chancellorsville. "The vacancies made by the death of Major-General Berry and Brigadier-General Whipple should, I respectfully suggest, be filled by promotion from the troops of the same army corps, considering that promotions have been so nobly earned in the corps." (OR, Vol. 51, Part I, pp. 1036-1037)

On December 8, 1863, General Prince's recommendation for the promotion of colonels Blaisdell and Brewster was forwarded by generals French and Meade. Prince and Blaisdell had served in the same regiment during the Mexican War, which is mentioned in a letter of recommendation of Blaisdell sent to General Humphreys by General Prince. Finally, there is a draft of a letter from General Humphreys to Senator Henry Wilson, dated March 4, 1864, strongly recommending Blaisdell as one who "has earned a high reputation for soldierly qualities," and citing his previous recommendations. (Humphreys Collection, Vol. 18) This would seem somewhat at odds with the editor's conclusion as to Blaisdell's status immediately preceding the reorganization and courts martial, although Humphreys' recommendation of the colonel at this time is somewhat mysterious.

68. McAllister letters, p. 401
69. Marbaker, pp. 154-155
70. Agassiz, George R., ed., *Meade's Headquarters, 1863-1865: Letters of Col. Theordore Lyman from the Wilderness to Appomattox,* 1922 (Atlantic Monthly Press), pp. 65-66 *(Hereinafter* Lyman)
71. *Ibid,* pp. 66-67
72. Humphreys Biography, p. 215
73. Davis, Oliver, *Life of David Bell Birney,* 1867 (Philadephia: King & Baird), p. 208 *(Hereinafter* Life of Birney)
74. Hall, Clark B., "Season of Change—The Winter Encampment of the Army of the Potomac", *Blue and Gray,* January 1989, p. 53
75. Blake, p. 271
76. Blake Memoirs, p. 53
77. *Ibid*
78. *Ibid.* Watson was dismissed by Special Order #90, AGO, U.S. War Dept., February 23, 1864.
79. On March 4, Gen. Meade submitted a reorganization plan to Gen. Halleck, which he approved and sent to Secretary Stanton. It, too, would have eliminated the I and III corps, but not as the approved plan. The I Corps divisions would have gone to the II Corps. The Kearny and Hooker Divisions (1st and 2nd) would have been combined and transferred to the V Corps. The 3rd Division of III Corps would have gone to the VI Corps, which was the only part of the plan carried out. (OR, Vol. 33, pp. 638-639) Why the original plan was scrapped is not apparent. Combining the old divisions of the III Corps would have created a much larger division than

any in either the II or V corps. And on the question of what corps got which divisions, perhaps Hancock, who had seniority over the V Corps's Gen. Gouverneur K. Warren, asked specifically for the III Corps divisions.

80. Hays, Gilbert A., *Under the Red Patch: Story of the 63rd Pennsylvania Volunteers,* 1908 (Pittsburgh: 63rd Pennsylvania Regimental Association), p. 222

81. Blake Memoirs, pp. 49-50

82. *The Virginia Campaign of '64 and '65,* 1883 (New York: Charles Scribner's Sons), p. 3 *(Hereinafter* Virginia Campaign) See also "Opening of the Campaign of 1864" (Massachusetts Historical Society, Vol. IV, p. 6) Meade's philosophy of "larger and fewer" went to brigades as well as corps. On March 25, the three brigades of the old 2nd division, III Corps were consolidated into two brigades in the new 4th Division of the II Corps. Under the new arrangement there were 9 and 8 regiments in the new 1st and 2nd brigades, respectively, of the 4th Division. The new 3rd Division (Birney) also had only two brigades, each composed of eight regiments and the U.S. Sharpshooters. (See Appendix A for location of the veteran III Corps regiments after realignment.) The old II Corps divisions of generals Francis Barlow and John Gibbon had four and three brigades, respectively, to some degree reflecting their greater numbers. There were fewer regiments per brigade in Barlow's four-brigade division, while in Gibbon's three-brigade division two of the brigades had eight or nine regiments. Dr. Richard Sommers of the U.S. Army Military Institute believes that "heavying up" the brigades in the Army of the Potomac reflected what already had taken place in the West, considered necessary because the reduced strengths of regiments in the army. This may have played a role in General Grant's support of Meade's reorganization. The corps in the west, however, were generally much smaller than the corps of the Army of the Potomac which in May 1864 had roughly 25,000 men. An exception to this would be Gen. John Scofield's XXIII Corps in the West, but it had five divisions. Moreover, unlike the 3rd and 4th division of the II Corps, the western divisions had at least three brigades.

The Confederate divisions generally had more brigades with fewer regiments. For instance, Henry Heth's division facing Mott and Birney in the Wilderness on May 5 had five brigades, four with four regiments and one with five.

It is interesting that General William Tecumseh Sherman, in his chapter on "Military Lessons of the War" believed that regiments should contain roughly 1200 soldiers in twelve companies and three battalions. "which in practice would settle down to about one thousand men." He noted that leaving recruiting to the States resulted in great variation in the size of regiments. Some did not keep the old regiment up to strength and formed new regiments. "We estimated a Wisconsin regiment (which kept its regiment up to strength) equal to an ordinary brigade." In Sherman's view, three regiments should constitute a brigade, three brigades a division and three divisions a corps. "Then, by allowing to an infantry corps a brigade of cavalry and six batteries of field-artillery, we would have an efficient *corps d'armeé* of thirty thousand men, whose organization would be simple and most efficient, and whose strength should never be allowed to fall below twenty-five thousand men." [Sherman, W.T., *Memoirs, Vol. 2.*, 1892 (New York: Charles L. Webster & Co.) pp. 384-385]

83. Webb, Alexander S., "Through the Wilderness", *Battles and Leaders of the Civil War, Vol. IV*, 1952 (New York: Thomas Yoseloff), p. 152

84. *Massachusetts Historical Society Papers, Vol. IV*, p. 224

85. McAllister letters, p. 402

86. Cudworth, pp. 449-452, his discussion of the reorganization

87. Judge Advocate General files, National Archives, Col. McLaughlen's court martial

88. McAllister letters, pp. 399-400

89. *Ibid*, p. 401

90. Walker, p. 400

91. Fleming, G. T., ed., *Life and Letters of Alexander Hays*, 1919 (Pittsburg), p. 562 *(Hereinafter* Hays letters). The "vision" quote is from Shakespeare's *The Tempest.*

92. *Ibid*, p. 560

93. *Ibid*, p. 571

94. Hutchinson, p. 12

95. McAllister letters, p. 402

96. U.S. Army, Office of the Judge Advocate General files, Record Group 153, court martial transcripts, National Archives, Washington, D.C. All subsequent quotes of trial proceedings are from transcripts unless otherwise indicated, including files NN 1534 (Bigelow), NN 1615 (Blake), NN 1579 (Forrest), NN 232 (Smith), NN 1615 (Smith), and NN 1615 (Thomas)

97. Blake Memoirs, pp. 73-74

98. Scott, Robert Garth, ed., *Fallen Leaves, The Civil War Letters of Major Henry Livermore Abbott*, 1991 (Kent, Ohio: Kent University Press), pp. 219-220 *(Hereinafter* Abbott letters)

99. The points of law were argued by both counsels citing William C. DeHart's *Observations on Military Law and the Constitution and Practive of Courts Martial with a Summary of the Law of Evidence* (1864, D. Appleton, New York). He is also the authority for the seating in the drawing of the court martial scene.

100. DuPaget, Alfred, *Military Service Record,* National Archives. Right after Chancellorsville, Col. McAllister wrote this to his wife: "This

Sunday's fight [May 3, 1863] is said to be the hardest battle of the war. and there in the very hottest part of it I stood with the gallant 11th—with the enemy on my front and right flank pouring into my ranks the balls, large and small, of death and destruction. Amidst it all there could be seen the Star-Spangled Banner and our State Colors, standing erect though riddled to pieces. Both flag staffs were broken by the shots of enemy. Undaunted, our brave and gallant colorbearer, DuPaget and his guard, bore them along in towards the enemy's lines. Then their forces would drive us back, a short distance only. As soon as we could get to the left and rear of the enemy's flank, we would pour into them our grape and ball, rally again around our standards, and on, on to the charge." (McAllister letters, p. 297)

101. Captain Allen was tried on March 27 for striking a Lt. Dickerson, quarter-master of the 26th Pennsylvania, and calling him a son-of-a-bitch on March 3rd, at a brigade ball. Provocation was a major issue and whether the ladies present heard the goings-on in a supply room adjacent to the hall, with Allen claiming that the "band played on." Strangely, the judge advocate at the trial was Lt. Blake, and the presiding officer was Col. Napoleon Bonaparte McLaughlen. Equally strange was a legal memorandum in Lt. Blake's handwriting, but signed by Capt. Allen, questioning some of the court rulings on the admissability of evidence in a number of instances, citing DeHart. The conviction was approved by Gen. Carr, who had been in command of the division just a few days. The file also contains a letter from Capt. Allen to Senator Wilson dated later in 1864 referring to a petition "signed by all the returned officers of the old 11th Regt. asking that the sentence be revoked and that I may enter the service again—I have recommended for the majority of the 11th Battalion by Lt. Col. Rivers now in command of that Battalion." (LL2025) Allen was a founding member of the 11th Massachusetts and had been severely wounded at Chancellorsville.

To further confuse the situation, the Boston *Herald* of June 21, 1864, lists Captain Allen as one of the officers of the 11th Massachusetts returning from the war that day. Obviously, the 11th Massachusetts did not recognize the court martial.

102. Captain Cook, the brigade commissary officer, may not have needed the money. Blake tells how he (Blake) was detailed to that position in September 1862 when Gen. Robert Cowdin, formerly colonel of the 1st Mass., was temporarily in charge of the brigade. He had been in the position for three days when the clerk presented a requisition for him to sign for three barrels of whiskey. Blake declared, "I shall not sign a requisition for the brigade while I am Commissary, and no man will get a drop if I can prevent it." Cowdin was no McAllister. Blake wrote, "I was relieved forthwith and Lieutenant Cook of the Second New Hampshire Infantry was my successor, and had a fortune when the war ended. Thus, I

lost my golden opportunity the first time it knocked." (Blake Memoirs, p. 64)

103. McAllister letters, p. 401

104. Blake Memoirs, p. 73

105. Carr, Pvt. James H., *Military Service Record,* National Archives, Washington, D.C. There is also a letter in the file dated March 6, 1863, from "Near Falmouth," to First Brigade, 3rd Division, HQ, [no Corps number] from "Lt. J.H. Carr, Lt. and aide-de-camp," requesting permission to go to Washington to clear up "my pay account of over eight (8) months standing," which was interferring with his ability to get credit for commissary store purchases. The records do not give any other clues as to how Carr could have been both a lieutentant aide-de-camp and a private in 1863.

106. Blake, p. 317

107. Blake Memoirs, p. 73

108. Hays letters, p. 576

109. *Ibid,* p. 578

110. Blake Memoirs, p. 71

111. Blake, p. 273. The court martial in the morning was probably Captain Allen's.

112. Blake Memoirs, p. 72

113. *Ibid,* pp. 72-73

114. *Ibid,* p. 74

115. *Ibid,* pp. 74-75

116. U.S. Treasury, Second Audit

117. McAllister letters, p. 402

118. Paladin, Vivian A., ed., "Proper Bostonian, Purpose Pioneer, Memoirs of Henry N. Blake," *Montana Western History, Vol. 14, No. 4,* October 1964, p. 36. *(Hereinafter* Blake Montana Memoirs) Blake was not particularly interested in promotions for a rather strange reason: "I never made any effort for promotion because I did not intend to join the Regular Army and for a singular reason which may appear absurd. I was bitten in my left hand by a horse when ten years old and never felt easy near the head or feet of the friend of man. I think I performed my duty as a soldier when standing on earth, and my conduct under fire was not censured, but I lost the feeling of confidence when mounted and the bullets were flying under me. I rode on a horse whenever ordered . . . but was happier when relieved and enjoyed the use of my feet." The validity of Blake's promotion to captain was also challenged and his records were generally confused in that he was mustered out with other veterans while being carried as wounded-sick.

119. Blake, p. 84. "I mention the last item because a disposition has been shown by certain parties to magnify the action of General Hancock in this engagement and deprive Gen. Hooker of that credit which he had so well

merited. Neither Gen. Hancock, nor the officers of men in his brigade, ever made any claim of this character, but took the opposite ground, and refused to accept the meed of praise they deserved." General Hancock should have remembered the 11th Massachusetts since General Sickles had lent it to Hancock during the first day at Chancellorsville and both commanders had complimented its performance in their reports on the battle.

120. DeTrobriand, pp. 658-659
121. *Ibid*, p. 669
122. *Ibid*
123. OR, Vol. 33, p. 1025. Francis Walker describes Gen. Gersholm Mott as "a very genial gentleman, perfectly brave, with much of the natural instinct of leadership, lacking perhaps in that stirring ambition which brings into their highest activity the qualities of a commander, but withal one who, as man or soldier, is never to be mentioned without respect." (Walker, p. 558)
124. General Hays, in a letter to his wife at the time of the reorganization, quotes a member of the Garibaldi Guards who, when he heard the rumor that Hays was once again going to be their commander, said, "H-ll, old Hays is coming back and there won't be a man of us alive." (Hays letters, p. 562)
125. Lyman, pp. 93
126. *Ibid*, pp. 114-115
127. *Morning Report of Co. K, 11th Massachusetts Volunteer Infantry,* May 1864 (Boston: Massachusetts Historical Society Collection) *(Hereinafter* Morning Report)
128. Hays letters, p. 578
129. Abbott letters, p. 146
130. Schaff, Morris, *The Battle of the Wilderness,* 1910 (Boston: Houghton Mifflin), p. 62 *(Hereinafter* Schaff)
131. Blake, p. 278
132. *Ibid*, pp. 276-277
133. Grant, U.S., *Personal Memoirs,* 1886 (New York: Charles Webster Co.), ol. II, p. 191 *(Hereinafter* Grant)
134. Blake, p. 277
135. Walker, p. 408
136. Schaff, pp. 59-60
137. Walker, pp. 411-412
138. Steere, Edward, *The Wilderness Campaign,* 1960 (Stackpole Press), pp. 187-188 *(Hereinafter* Steere) A shorter, more readable work, well illustrated and mapped is *Into the Wilderness with the Army of the Potomac,* 1988 (University of Indiana Press) by Robert Garth Scott.
139. *Ibid*, p. 188

140. Walker, p. 414
141. Blood, Samuel L., *Military Service Record,* National Archives
142. Blake, pp. 279-280
143. Schaff, pp. 39-40
144. Hancock, Winfield Scott, "Report on 2nd Corps Operations, May 3rd to May 7, 1864", OR Vol 36, Part I, p. 327
145. Walker, p. 398
146. Blake, pp. 278-279
147. OR, Vol. 36, Part II, pp. 409-410
148. Steere, p. 189
149. OR, Vol. 36, Part II, p. 410
150. Steere, pp. 199-200
151. In Col. Brewster's military file is a letter which states that "in the present campaign he participated the first day of the Wilderness fight when he was taken sick and remained in hospital until May 28 when he reported for duty." This explains a previously seemingly mysterious communication to Mott's headquarters signed by William Blaisdell, colonel commanding brigade, stating, "I have posted the pickets as ordered. We connect with General Ward [Birney] . . . and on the left with Colonel Smyth, commanding brigade Second Corps [Barlow] 4:30 May 5." (OR, Vol. 36, Part II, p. 412) [Blake, p. 279]
152. OR, Vol. 36, Part I, p. 498
153. Cudworth, pp. 459-460
154. OR, Vol. 36, Part I, p. 488
155. *Ibid,* pp. 503-504
156. *Ibid,* p. 122
157. Lyman, pp. 91-92
158. Steere, p. 211
159. Walker, pp. 416-418
160. Grant, p. 194
161. Blake, p. 275
162. Lyman, pp. 92-93
163. Abbott letters, pp. 188-189
164. Page, Charles D., *History of the Fourteenth Regiment Connecticut Volunteer Infantry,* 1906 (Meriden, Conn.: Horton Printing Co.), p. 219 *(Hereinafter* 14th Conn.)
165. 14th Conn., pp. 221-222
166. Hays letters, p. 594
167. *Ibid,* p. 552. In a letter to his wife on March 27th, Gen. Hays listed his full animal complement: "I have Secessia and Solomon, besides two fine extra horses, allowed me by orders. I have my excellent and admired spring wagon, with the two sorrel horses of your acquaintance, but as fat as seals; for heavy transportation two six-mule teams, and for immediate provision my own pet

mule, Puss, with Edwin as trainmaster and cook. Peggy and Crumpy [cows] will bring up the rear. I have a churn, and have turned dairyman." (Hays letters, p. 566)

168. Fatout, Paul, ed., *Watson, Maj. William, Letters of a Civil War Surgeon,* 1962, (Purdue University Studies) p. 81

169. Catton, Bruce, *A Stillness at Appomattox,* 1953 (Garden City, N.Y.: Doubleday & Co.) p. 75

170. Cudworth, p. 460

171. Blake, p. 281

172. Steere, p. 361

173. OR, Vol. 36, Part I, pp. 488-489

174. Steere, p. 362

175. Hays letters, p. 581

176. OR, Vol. 36, Part I, p. 321

177. *Ibid*, p. 489

178. Steere, p. 395

179. OR, Vol. 36, Part I, p. 489

180. Blake, pp. 281-282

181. Steere, p. 399-400

182. Abbott letters, p. 5

183. Schaff, p. 259

184. Lyman, pp. 94-95

185. *Ibid*, p. 97. Colonel George Macy rejoined the 20th Mass. the night of May 5 and replaced Abbott as its commanding officer. His tenure was less than a day, and Abbott was again commanding at his fatal wounding.

186. Smith, J. D., *The History of the 19th Maine Regiment of Voluntary Infantry,* 1909. (Minneapolis: Great Western Printing Co.), pp. 141-143

187. Steere, p. 403

188. *Ibid*, p. 409

189. Blake, pp. 282-283

190. Steere, p. 419

191. Blake, p. 283

192. Steere, p. 423

193. Blake, p. 283

194. Steere, pp. 423-425

195. Blake, pp. 283-284

196. OR, Vol. 36, Part I, p. 504

197. *Ibid*, pp. 489-490

198. McAllister letters, p. 416

199. Schaff, pp. 292-293

200. OR, Vol. 36, Part II, p. 446

201. Lyman, p. 97

202. OR, Vol. 36, Part I, p. 354
203. Morning Report
204. Fox, William F., *Regimental Losses in the American Civil War,* 1889 (Albany Publishing Co.), p. 159 *(Hereinafter* Regimental Losses) I am sure Blake and a lot of the members of the Hooker Brigade would have had grave reservations with Fox's designation of them as being in Carr's Brigade and Humphrey's Division, their Gettysburg configuration. Fox is not consistent, as he designates the New York regiments of the Excelsior as Sickles' Brigade and Hooker's Division. Of course, the double Hooker designation would seem odd, but the Old Brigade veterans might have appreciated being designated at least as the Grover Brigade, Hooker Division.
205. Walker, pp. 438-439
206. Blake, p. 285
207. *Ibid*
208. *Ibid,* p. 286
209. *Ibid,* pp. 286-287
210. *Ibid,* p. 287
211. *Ibid*
212. *Ibid,* pp. 287-288
213. Matter, William D., *If It Takes All Summer, the Battle of Spotsylvania,* 1988 (Chapel Hill: University of North Carolina Press), p. 160 *(Hereinafter* Matter)
214. Walker, p. 461
215. Humphreys Virginia Campaign, pp. 86-87
216. Walker, p. 463
217. *Ibid*
218. Matter, pp. 160-161
219. OR, Vol. 36, Part I, p. 490
220. Matter states that "apparently" Blaisdell was in charge of the brigade on May 10 and that Mott seems to have stayed at the Brown house during the attack. (pp. 160-161) Oliver Wendell Holmes, Jr., who was on Gen. Horatio Wright's VI Corps staff, wrote that he was sent to outline the route of Mott's attack at 11 A.M. and found him "somewhat stupid and flurried." [Howe, Mark De Wolfe, ed. *Touched with Fire-Civil War Letters and Diary,* 1947. (Harvard University Press), p. 111 *(Hereinafter* Holmes Letters)]
221. McAllister letters, p. 417
222. Foote, Shelby, *The Civil War, A Narrative, Vol. 3, Red River to Appomattox,* 1974, (New York: Random House), p. 209 *(Hereinafter* Foote Vol. 3)
223. Blake, pp. 289-290
224. Foote, Vol. 3, p. 213
225. Walker, p. 470

226. *Ibid,* p. 471
227. OR, Vol. 36, Part I, p. 505
228. Walker, p. 471
229. Blake, pp. 290-291
230. Old Harvard Soldier, p. 1060
231. OR, Vol. 36, Part I., p. 491. Walker described Merriam as "an accomplished and graceful gentleman, a brave and intelligent soldier." (Walker, pp. 476-477)
232. Matter, p. 186
233. *Ibid*
234. *Ibid,* pp. 253-254
235. Walker, p. 479
236. Blake, p. 291
237. *Ibid,* p. 292. Blake also advised why press accounts should be viewed with some scepticism. "The correspondents of the newspapers eagerly questioned the staff-officers to ascertain the details of the battle which they had not witnessed; and by this means I obtained a knowledge of the origin of many untruthful items,—that Gen. This saved the day at one point, and Gen. That at another time turned defeat into victory." (Blake, pp. 292-293)
238. OR, Vol. 36, Part I, p. 359
239. OR, Vol. 36, Part I, p. 218: "Medical Director's Report, Army of the Potomac" *(Hereinafter* Medical Report *with OR page numbers)*
240. *Ibid,* p. 220
241. Blake, pp. 291-292
242. Blake Memoirs, p. 63
243. Medical Report, p. 225
244. U.S. War Department, Medical and Surgical History of the Civil War, Vol. 2, p. 614
245. Blake, pp. 293-294
246. *Ibid,* p. 294. Blake's account after the war also notes that their defrocked chaplain now working for the Christian Commission "was a friend in need and assisted me and my friends of the 11th who were suffering from wounds by appropriating for our benefit all the supplies he could carry." (Blake Memoirs, p. 54)
247. *Ibid,* pp. 294-295
248. Blake Memoirs, p. 73
249. Blake, p. 296
250. Medical Report, p. 220
251. *Ibid,* p. 221
252. Military and Pension Service File, National Archives, Washington, D.C.
253. Walker, p. 481
254. Morning Report

255. Hutchinson, p. 69
256. *Ibid*
257. Hunt, Roger D. and Jack R. Brown, *Brevet Brigadier Generals in Blue,* 1990 (Gaithersburg, Md.: Olde Soldier Books), p. vii *(Hereinafter* Brevets in Blue)
258. Blake Memoirs, p. 62
259. *Ibid.* In Walker's book (opposite p. 540) there is a map of the siege of Petersburg which shows the Union forts named for its deceased heroes. Fort Blaisdell (on the Jerusalem Plank Road) is near Fort Alexander Hays.
260. Bruce, George A., *The 20th Regiment of Massachusetts Volunteer Infantry,* 1906 (Boston: Houghton Mifflin and Co.), p. 356 *(Hereinafter* 20th Mass.)
261. *Ibid,* p. 357
262. Abbott letters, p. 16
263. 20th Mass., p. 357
264. Abbott letters, p. 1
265. *Ibid*
266. *Ibid,* p. 255 The preservation of reverence for Little Abbott and his contemporaries, largely though the words and thought of Justice Holmes, had inter-generational overtones. I remember Paul Freund in a constitutional law course at Harvard Law School in 1950 lecturing on this phenomenon and stating to our class, a high proportion of whom were somewhat cynical veterans of World War II, that Holmes' writing on the war had an element of "schmaltz" but that it was "magnificent schmaltz." The Holmesian spirit, characterized by another statement in the Memorial Day address "through our great good fortune, in our youth our hearts were touched with fire," (Holmes letters, p. vi) was carried forward by his law clerks, one of whom, Arthur E. Sutherland, was influential in my decision to leave his seminar at Harvard and reenter the service in the Korean War.
267. Hays letters, p. 649
268. *Ibid*
269. National Archives, Adjutant Generals Office (AGO) files
270. National Archives, Military Service Record
271. *Ibid*
272. Blake Montana Memoirs, p. 36
273. *Ibid*
274. Blake, p. iii
275. National Archives, AGO files
276. Brevets in Blue, p. 275
277. U.S. Archives, Military Service and Pension Records
278. *Ibid*
279. 19th Maine, p. 303; Brevets in Blue, p. 582
280. Walker, p. 684

281. Medal of Honor Awards, 1863-1963, U.S. Senate Labor and Public Welfare Committee Print, p. 378. The file in the National Archives shows that the original application for the medal noted Bingham's performance in a number of actions. It was rejected with a notation that it be based on "conspicuous gallantry" in a particular battle and the revised application specified the Wilderness. Such a late award would be prohibited under current procedures which place a time limit of three years between the event and the award. The award, however, did pass the scrutiny of the Congressional Medal review board, which was convened a few years after Bingham's death to weed out undeserving recipients of our highest award for bravery in battle.
282. McAllister letters, p. 427
283. *Ibid*, p. 468
284. *Ibid*, p. 16
285. *Daily Times*
286. *Ibid*
287. *Ibid*
288. Blake Memoirs, p. 46; pp. 67-68
289. Abbott letters, pp. 3, 11
290. Blake, p. 282
291. Records of Jeane Elizabeth (Blood) Rines and Russell Blood, Saugus, Massachusetts.
292. Blake Memoirs, pp. 319-321
293. *Ibid*, p. 321
294. *Ibid*, pp. 321-322
295. Swanberg, p. 390
296. McAllister letters, p. 16
297. Blake Memoirs, p. 73
298. Bingham, Henry Harrison, "Memorial Address in House and Senate", House Doc. 956, 62nd Congress
299. Rensselaer County, New York, Historical Society, "Profile of Major-General Joseph Bradford Carr"
300. Blake Montana Memoirs, p. 37
301. *Ibid*, p. 38
302. *Ibid*
303. *Ibid*
304. *Ibid*, p. 39
305. *Ibid*
306. *Ibid*, p. 38
307. *Ibid*, p. 39
308. *Ibid*, p. 40
309. *Ibid*

310. *Ibid*

311. *Ibid*

312. *Ibid*

313. Warner, Ezra J., *Generals in Blue*, (Baton Rouge: Louisiana University Press) p. 318

314. Blake Montana Memoirs, p. 41

315. *Ibid*, p. 42

316. *Ibid*, p. 44

317. *Ibid*, p. 44-45

318. *Ibid*, p. 50

319. *Ibid*, p. 51

320. Justice Holmes was also a competitor to Blake in longevity. He outlived Blake, dying at age 91 on March 6, 1935, but he was younger by about four years. Holmes entered Harvard University in 1857 and graduated from the law school in 1866.

321. Virginia Campaign, p. 55

322. W. H. Wheeler Manuscripts, Perkins Library, Duke University

323. Blake Memoirs, p. 38

324. McAllister letters, pp. 519-521

325. Walker, p. 632

326. McAllister letters, pp. 521-522

327. DeTrobriand, p. 668

328. McAllister letters, p. 409

329. *Daily Times*, p. 8. The article quotes a letter which Humphreys wrote to Congressman John A. Griswold, representing Troy. "[A]t Gettysburg [Carr] was close to me repeatedly, and constantly under observation during the hottest of the battle. I do not know a braver or cooler man." No draft of this letter was found in the collection of the Historical Society of Pennsylvania.

330. Humphreys Biography, p. 179

331. *Ibid*, p. 180

332. *Ibid*, pp. 183-184

333. *Ibid*, p. 184

334. *Ibid*, pp. 186-187

335. *Ibid*, p. 201

336. *Ibid*, p. 205

337. *Ibid*, p. 219

338. *Ibid*

339. *Ibid*, p. 241

340. *Ibid*

341. Humphreys Collection. Right before the 1864 election, Humphreys was confident he would be given the II Corps when he wrote, "The Second

Corps will, however, be given to me unless the Secretary of War should oppose objection sufficiently strong to overrule General Grant with the President. . . . It is a high position and carries with it certain privileges, among them the appointment of Aides-de-Camp with additional rank so that —— would profit by it. There was evidently some hostility to me last winter and spring, the real source of which probably was some idea that I was what was called a strong McClellan man, an imputation that was offensive to me, as it affirmed that I was some man's man. In politics, I have all along taken no part, and I will not take part. I know not the political basis of any one even in the army, and I shall treat all attempts to induce me to take sides in the manner in which I treated those last winter. I would not yield one inch of my independent position and I came out with flying colors." (Humphreys Biography, p. 257)

342. Life of Birney, p. 242 Birney was the lawyer son of a former Southern slave-owner turned abolitionist. His elder brother, William, was even more active in organizing and leading colored troops. He was also brevetted as a major general.

343. *Ibid*, pp. 243-244

344. *Ibid*. Birney died on October 18, 1864, in Philadelphia of a malarial infection he had gotten in Virginia. One of his last acts was to vote in the election on October 11 while gravely ill. He told the author of his biography, "Well, I voted, and I have done all in my power to defeat these infernal copperheads, who have done more to prolong this rebellion than the rebels. Don't fail to do your duty to-day to your country. Vote as I have, or don't vote at all." (p. 277)

345. Lyman, p. 73

346. Carr had shown his political ability in advancing to a colonel in the New York militia over a ten year period before the war. Blake's only favorable comment on Carr was that he was "a fine drill master." (Blake Memoirs, p. 73) Blake wrote that "Charges of cowardice which were submitted by one division commander against another were repeatedly suppressed because the guilty person was a personal admirer and flatterer of the head of the army." (Blake, p. 317) Carr and Meade are identifiable, but whether the accusing brigadier general was Gen. Prince is less certain.

347. OR, Vol. 27, Part I, p. 544. But see note 329 quoting the Troy *Daily Times*.

348. Humphreys Collection. Walker notes that Gen. Humphreys was also capable of giving slights. Walker wrote that Humphreys, in his report and in a subsequent letter to William Swinton printed in his "Army of the Potomac", had been unfair to the II Corps divisions of Hancock and French in describing the assult on Marye's Heights at Fredericksburg. Humphreys had implied that the II Corps troops lying on the ground from the previous assaults were the reason his division did not carry the stone wall. Walker, though lavishly praising Humphrey's performance, said that it was the Confederate fire that was responsible for the failure and that the bodies of

soldiers from the Irish Brigade (Meagher) and Caldwell's Brigade, not Humphreys's Division, were those closest to the wall. (Walker, pp. 185-187)

349.   Gen. Carr was very briefly in command of an XVIII Corps division at the time of the Burnside mine explosion episode, but the division was not in action.

A Commentary on the Cited Sources

*(Ed. Note: Detailed bibliographic information for all sources
may be found at their initial listing in the notes.)*

It is obvious that the writings of Captain Blake have played a dominant role in the development of this book. These include *Three Years in the Army of the Potomac,* now out-of-print, and his memoirs, some published and some unpublished.

Blake's book has been somewhat neglected by Civil War writers over the years, but his colorful language and cutting commentary are beginning to appear in some major books. John Hennessy, in his definitive study entitled *Return to Bull Run: The Campaign and Battle of Second Manassas,* published this year (1993), includes Blake's evaluation of Gen. John Pope's performance as representative of that of the rank and file. Blake called Pope a "dunderpate" and said his command could have been more effectively executed "by intelligent sergeants." Blake is also one of the sources for Hennessey's extensive description of Gen. Grover's bayonet charge on Stonewall Jackson's troops at the railroad embankment at Groveton.

Harry W. Pfanz, in *Gettysburg—The Second Day,* records Blake's use of the more modern expression of "blockhead" in describing Gen. Carr's performance at Gettysburg. When Blake was emphasizing the cowardly aspects of Carr he was "a starred poltroon" or an "arrant" coward. Noah Trudeau, in his 1989 book *Bloody Roads South,* includes Blake's description of a Union colonel's (Blaisdell) treatment of Union "skulkers" on the first day of the Wilderness and Blake's account of how the "myrmidons" of Longstreet advanced on his picket line at the Brock-Plank Road crossing on the second day.

Scant use of Blake as a source in the past is possibly due to the nature of *Three Years in the Army of the Potomac,* written in late 1864 and early 1865, and which has an air of mystery to it. Blake notes that he does not "mention by name the officers and enlisted men of his regiment although some of their heroic acts are briefly described." Neither does Blake give the names of certain generals he "was compelled to serve under." The reader must figure out the corps, division or brigade commander at the time of the reference and relate this individual to the pertinent insult Even so, this approach, which he denied was based on fear of possible litigation, was quite courageous in 1865, for his characterization of Gen. Carr seemed libelous on its face unless the defense of truth could be successfully made. (Blake's least admired generals list includes Irvin McDowell, William B. Franklin, Andrew A. Humphreys [whom he mistakenly calls Alfred], William H. French, and Joseph B. Carr.)

In his various postwar memoirs, Blake attaches more names. The unpublished memoirs were obtained piecemeal, but they are all based on an account that Blake wrote in 1916, some 300 pages typewritten by his daughter as his wife read his handwritten manuscript. The Western (Montana) History article was prepared from this typescript in 1964; I obtained a copy from that state's historical society. Inquiry at the Harvard and Harvard Law School libraries unearthed a brief article in the Harvard Alumni Bulletin of June 16, 1927, "Tales By An Old Harvard Soldier," that describes his law school and war experiences.

It seemed to me that there was possibly additional information in the 1916 typewritten draft, and I was fortunate in getting Blake's great granddaughter, Patricia Ernsberger, to send me all the pages of the memoirs relating to the war. These pages provided descriptions of a number of incidents relevant to the story and gave greater insight into the courts martial and the major players in the drama.

Col. Robert McAllister's official reports are some of the most extensive of any middle grade Union officer in the Civil War. They have been used extensively by historians over the years. The official reports are supplemented by his voluminous letters, edited and arranged skillfully by Prof. James I. Robertson, Jr., in 1965. They directly bear upon the acrimonious in-fighting at Brandy Station in 1863-1864, the reorganization, courts martial and its aftermath in the Wilderness and Spotsylvania. Similarly, the letters of Gen. Alexander Hays and Major Henry Abbott, which continue up to a few days before their deaths in the Wilderness, were also invaluable in enhancing our understanding of the courts martial board and the men who served upon it. The Abbott letters, *Fallen Leaves,* edited by Robert Garth Scott, were published in 1991; the Hays letters were published over 70 years ago.

Index

ambulances, 123
amputations, 137
Anderson, G.T., 118, 120
Anderson, Richard H., 122, 128
Andrew, John A., 30
Appropriations Committee (House), 162
Arcola, Va. (See Gum Springs, Va.)
Army of the Potomac, xv, 43, 176; training in, 84

B

Barlow, Francis C., 89-91, 100, 105, 107, 109, 115, 117, 120, 128-129, 131
Bartlett, A.W., 10, 12
Batchelder, John B., 93
Battles
  Balls Bluff, 111, 144
  Big Bethel, 4
  Boydton Plank Road, 81, 141, 151, 169-173
  Bull Run, 1st battle of, 1, 3, 155
  Bull Run, 2nd battle of, 1, 3, 6
  Chancellorsville, xviii, 1-2, 54, 57, 86, 135, 154, 175, 189
  Cold Harbor, 140, 142
  Farmville, 150
  Fredericksburg, 144, 154, 174, 176
  Gettysburg, 1, 16, 20, 93, 101, 144, 154, 179; casualties, 121
  Glendale, 144
  High Bridge (Appomattox), 149
  Mine Run campaign, 25-26, 31, 43, 174
  North Anna, 140, 142
  Peninsula campaign, 1
  Spotsylvania, 31, 74, 81-83, 122-142; Salient, xviii, 126-128, 130-131, 133; Upton's assault, 124-125 route of attack, 131-132
  Totopotomoy Creek, 140
  Wilderness, xviii, 43-44, 81, 83, 84-98, 104-120, 155, 195; care of wounded, 135; casualties, 121; failure to use artillery, 100, 116-117; lack of artillery, 137; lack of reports on, 94; "show blood" test, 92; use of cavalry, 109
  Williamsburg, 79-80
Baxter, Henry, 109
Bealeton, Va., 12

Belle-Plain Landing, 138
Belvedere, N.J., 161
Benning, Henry L., 107
Berry, Hiram, 2, 24
Beverly Ford, 9-10
Bigelow, James R., 46, 49, 69-70, 72, 78-79, 82; court martial, 53-57, 59-62, 64, 66-67; postwar, 146
Bingham, Henry H., 49, 54, 59, 61-62, 64, 68, 77, 83, 133, 149, 172; Medal of Honor, 150; postwar, 161-162; wounded, 139
Birney, David B., 14, 24-25, 38, 41, 44, 82, 84, 89-91, 95-96, 99, 105-108, 112, 114-116, 120, 128-129, 140, 151, 155, 177-179, 197
Birney, William, 197
Black Horse Tavern, 15
Blaisdell, William, xviii, 23, 28-29, 33, 40-41, 47, 49, 59, 61, 63, 67, 72, 82, 92, 94, 126, 133, 154, 190; denied promotion, 30-32; lauded by Blake, 32; Mexican War with Grant, 143; on Bigelow, 54; prewar military experience, 30; promoted, 142; relationship with McAllister, 27; use of alcohol, 28, 31-32
Blake, Henry N., 2-4, 12, xvii-xviii, 46, 54, 77, 82-83, 92, 94, 106, 110, 115, 148, 153, 158, 162, 170, 188; 1st court martial, 22-23; 2nd court martial, 60, 66-68, 71-72; 50th reunion of Hooker Brigade, 156; appointed to Montana supreme court, 167; challenged to duel, 165; court martial, 70; death of, 159, 168; loses brother, 154; meeting with Sen. Wilson, 42-43; on Blaisdell, 30, 32; on Carr, 6, 9, 16; on Hancock, 79; on Hays, 101; on Meade, 122-123; on the military justice system, 63; on the reliability of press reports, 193; on treatment of wounded, 135-136; on Union medical operations, 138-139; political opinion, 55-56; postwar, 162-165, 167-168; postwar, Montana, 72, 148, 163-165, 167-168; on supreme court, 167; promoted to captain, 79; returns to Boston, 168; view on alcohol, 31; view on religion, 38-40; wounded, 130, 138; writes book, 147

110, 112, 114, 116, 120, 145
Point Lookout Prison, 7, 9
Post Offices & Post Roads Committee
(House), 162
Prince, Henry, 24-26, 28, 46, 76

R

Rapidan River, xviii
Rappahannock; crossing of (1863), 9
Rappahannock Station, 135
reorganization of the army, xvii, 26, 41, 44,
57, 140, 153; criticized, 43, 48, 51-52;
Kearny-Birney Div. erects "headstone",
41; protest meeting, 45, 50, 59, 64;
resolution, 50; rationale, 43
Rice, James C., 114, 119-120
Ricketts, James, 41
Rivers, Charles C., 64-65, 78, 83, 151, 170,
173
Robertson's Tavern, 89
Rockhill, William S., 58, 61, 69, 71, 73,
77-78, 147
Rogers Farmhouse, 16-17; 156, 158
Rogers, Peter, 156
Russell, Levi S., 64

S

Scales, Albert, 104
Schaff, Morris, 87, 92, 111
Schofield, John, 185
Schoonover, John, 48-49, 63, 73, 77, 119,
155
Scott, Winfield, 30
Sedgwick, John, 34, 87, 144
Sewell, William J., 109
Shady Grove Church, 89
Sickles, Daniel, 2, 14-15, 24, 30, 76,
156-159, 179, 189
skulkers, 94
Sleeper, Samuel T., 58, 60-61, 69, 73, 77,
83; killed, 133
Smith, John H.,59, 64, 74, 78
Smith, Walter N., 46, 72; 1st court martial,
75-76; 2nd court martial, 73-75; prewar, 75
Smyth, Thomas A., 109, 190
Soldiers Rest Hospital, Boston, 140
Southside Railroad, 169
Sowter, John, 74, 78

Spotswood, Alexander, 85
Stanton, Edwin M., 81, 148
Starbird, Isaac, 51, 53-54, 104, 112, 149
Steuart, George H., 127-129, 134
Stevenson, Thomas G., 107
Stone, Benjamin, 3, 138
Stone, Martin, 20, 23
Stuart, James E. B., 6
Sumner, Charles, 30, 55
Sunbright, 37-38
Sutherland, Arthur E., 194

T

Teaffle, William, 64-65, 83
Thomas Edward C., 46, 59, 72; court
martial, 78-79
Thompson, Thomas C., 96
Thoroughman, Thomas, 165
Three Years in the Army of the Potomac, 3,
199-200
Todd's Tavern, 89, 122
Tripp, Porter D., 23, 40, 75
Troy, N.Y., 162
Turnbull, John C., 16

U

U.S. Army General Hospital, Readville,
Mass., 140
Upton, Emory, 124-126, 132

V

Vigilantes, 163-164
Virginia City, Mont., 168

W

Wadsworth, James, 106-107, 110-112, 114
Walker, Francis, 24, 47-48, 90-91, 94,
99-100
Walker, Henry H., 97
Ward, J.H. Hobart, 96, 119, 190
Warren, Gouveneur K., 26, 87, 95, 169, 185
Warrenton Junction, 10-11, 22
Watson, Elisha F., 40
Webb, Alexander S., 43, 85, 101, 104, 107,
112, 114, 143
Welling, E.C., 56
Wheeler, W.H., 169
White, Rufus A., 63, 65, 83

About the Author

Fred Arner, an attorney, was educated at Kenyon College, the George Washington Law School and the Harvard Law School. He worked for the Congressional Research Service and as Committee staff on social security and medicare legislation for more than thirty years and is the author of a book and several articles on these subjects. He served as a tail gunner in a B-29 in the air offensive against Japan during World War II and as a chief gunner on a B-36 in the Strategic Air Command during the Korean War.